When the Bottom Drops Out of Your Life

JUNE E. BENNETT

When the Bottom Drops Out of Your Life
Cover design by Maja Kopunovic Legetin

ACKNOWLEDGMENTS

With special thanks:

To God, for the things He has done and continues to do in each of our lives. Never did He leave nor forsake me.

To the awesome pastors and wonderful people at ALMs, a small community church with the heart and love of God flowing in abundance. Thank you for going much more than the extra mile with my family.

To the friends and neighbors who knew us, stood by us, and helped beyond measure. Your kindness will always be remembered.

To Ginny, Sandi, Venesia, Lavern and many, many other wonderful sisters in the Lord. I'm certain God put you in my life "for such a time as this." The load was easier to bear because of each of you.

To all the intercessors for standing in the gap for us and doing some serious warfare on our behalf; especially to Barbara and Belinda.

To my children, who have shown unconditional love and continuously encouraged me to write this book. All my love; you are truly my jewels.

TABLE OF CONTENTS

PREFACE

It has taken me close to a decade to complete this writing. At first it was just too painful because in writing it I had to relive it. Sometimes, when I tried to write, it felt as if a wound that was trying to heal was being scraped open again. Initially, I did not want to write this story because some part of me wanted to forget it ever happened. However, the Holy Spirit continuously prompted me to write. There were times that I wrote and then put it down for months. There were times that tears ran like a river down my face as I wrote.

The Word of God tells us that confirmation comes from the mouth of two or three individuals. I received numerous confirmations that I needed to write because this was and is a unique story that needed to be told, and in the telling of it healing would come not only to me, but to others as well.

Still, I made lots of excuses to God, telling Him that I am not a professional writer, but the Lord would not accept any of my excuses, no matter how uncomfortable and painful it was. He reminded me that He doesn't necessarily call the qualified to do a job, but instead He qualifies those whom He calls. Moses didn't think he had the qualifications to lead the children of Israel out of the bondage of Egypt, but God called him, equipped him, and used him. There are numerous examples in the Bible of God calling people to do a task that they really didn't feel they had the skills to accomplish, but God gave them the skills needed for the task, and such has been the case for me in writing this book.

It is my great hope that as you read of this family's saga you will be encouraged to know God in a real and personal way, and to know that God is faithful and never leaves nor forsakes us, no matter how deep the valley, no matter how high the mountain, even when the bottom seems to drop totally out of your life, with irreversible, unthinkable, never to be forgotten events. God is always there! Truly, in the writing of this story the deep healing began for me, and still continues.

1

ON THE RUN

OCTOBER, 2003

Little did I realize that what began as a routine evening at home would be a night never to be forgotten. It would be the beginning of a season of great turmoil in our lives, and in the lives of many others, as well as a harbinger of things to come. Our lives would be forever changed, not so much by this night, but more accurately by the events which lead to the death of an eighteen-year-old young man, four months earlier, whom I had never met.

It was a clear, crisp October night and I was busily engaged in the necessary but mundane chores of a single working mother. I washed the after dinner dishes, folded laundry, and talked to my fifteen-year-old daughter, Julia about how her day had been at school. I was partially listening to Julia chat about the new, cute boy in one of her classes but my thoughts and prayers were for my oldest son, Matt, who had been gone almost two weeks. We didn't know where he was. We only knew he had left the area, and the police were looking for him. Matt was twenty-four years old and the oldest of my five children.

The phone rang abruptly, interrupting my thoughts and my conversation with Julia. It was Tom and Dorothy, friends whom we attended church with. They were in my neighborhood and said they needed to stop by for a few minutes. Our families had known each other almost twenty years. Their family also had five children. Minutes later the doorbell rang. As I greeted them the pained expression on Tom's face was too urgent too ignore. "What's wrong Tom? Is it one of your sons?" "It's not one of my sons this time, Diana. It's one of yours. It's Matt."

Tom had been a reporter for our local newspaper for many years. "Diana," Tom began, "as you may already be aware the police are looking for Matt in connection with a drug related home invasion robbery that occurred several months ago. An eighteen-year-old young man was shot and killed during the incident. I have been assigned to write an article which will appear in tomorrow morning's paper. It will go out on the Associated Press wire, throughout the United States. It will be front page news here in our area and will carry a picture of Matt. Dorothy and I felt we needed to come tell you, first-hand, before you see it in the paper tomorrow or you get a call from someone while you're at work."

"An eighteen-year-old is dead?! Oh my God! Is that why Matt has left the area?!" I felt as if I had been hit in the chest and needed a minute to catch my breath. Matt had most certainly been in trouble with the police, numerous times for petty issues, since he was about seventeen years old, but this…he could not possibly be involved in something as serious as the death of an eighteen year old! No way!!

Tom continued, "Diana, did you know anything about this? Did you see the story about the young man's death in the newspaper several months ago?" "No, Tom. This is the first time I am hearing of a home invasion and an eighteen-year-old being killed.

I spoke to Matt about two weeks ago on the phone. He told me he had to leave the area because he was going to be accused of a crime that he did not commit. I couldn't get any details out of him at that time. He was very upset and I could not reason with him. Apparently the police tried to arrest him for something. He eluded them and has left the area. I have no idea where he is."

As we continued to talk, I noticed an ambulance pulling into my driveway. Seconds later there were men in dark clothing jumping out of the back of the ambulance with what appeared to be weapons in their hands. A SWAT team!! At my house! Before I had time to wonder what was going on, our phone rang. "Mrs. Smith, this is Detective Jefferson, with the Sheriff's Department. Does your son, Matt, happen to be in your house?" "Matt is not here," I responded. "Mrs. Smith, please step out into the yard." Tom, Dorothy, and Julia remained in the house while I stepped out, and was immediately surrounded by the SWAT team. Detective Jefferson stepped forward, identifying himself with his badge. "Mrs. Smith, we'd like to come inside your home and have a look around to be certain Matt is not inside." "Yes, of course," I replied.

The SWAT team entered the house with weapons drawn. Some going upstairs, while others went downstairs. They asked for the key to a storage closet downstairs that I kept locked because it contained some of my daughter Joanna's clothing and her special things from college which Julia loved helping herself to, without her older sister's permission. The SWAT team went into every room of our house, looking under beds, in closets, and even pulling back the shower curtains in the bathrooms. When they were satisfied Matt was not there they went back outside.

Detective Jefferson and another detective who identified himself as Detective Ellis, along with Matt's probation officer, then entered the house and came into the living room, where Tom,

Dorothy, Julia and I sat. Detectives Jefferson and Ellis spoke to Tom, who had covered many of their cases. Turning to me Detective Jefferson asked, "Mrs. Smith, when have you last seen Matt?" "It's been about two weeks," I responded. "Mrs. Smith, did you know that he eluded us about two weeks ago?" "Yes, I knew that." "Do you happen to know where he is?" "No, I have no idea where he is." "And do you know why we're looking for your son, Mrs. Smith?" "I was just told by Tom, shortly before you arrived, that there was a drug related home invasion robbery several months ago and an eighteen-year-old young man was killed; but why do you suspect Matt of being involved?" "Matt's DNA was recovered from the crime scene," was Detective Ellis' stoic response. "I see," was all I could manage to say, as I choked back the tears of unbelief.

Detective Ellis asked if Matt actually lived here. "Well, although not physically," I began, "he still gets mail here and usually comes once a week to do his laundry, or have dinner with us, if he's in the area." "Where else does he stay?" asked Detective Ellis. "He sometimes stays with my ex-husband, Edward, who no longer lives in this area. He also shares a townhouse with another young man." Before leaving the detectives politely but firmly instructed me to contact the police immediately if I heard from Matt. As a mother I did not think I would be able to do that, but I nodded my head.

Tom and Dorothy stayed a while longer after the police left. Tom said he suspected some sort of bugging device had probably been placed in our house, and we could expect our telephone conversations would soon be monitored to find out if we were in contact with Matt. Before leaving Tom and Dorothy prayed with Julia and me. Our prayer was for Matt to quickly turn himself in, where ever he was.

Two weeks earlier, on the Friday evening Matt eluded the police, I tried calling him several times, but he wasn't answering his cell phone. He always answered calls from me. After numerous attempts to reach him, I felt something was wrong. I had called my friend Debbie and told her I just couldn't shake the feeling that something was terribly wrong with Matt. We prayed together for his protection, and for me to have peace, but even when I got off the phone with Debbie, I paced back and forth, praying in the spirit, and asking God to please protect Matt, wherever he was, and whatever he was doing.

Several hours after Debbie and I prayed, Matt called. It was not good. He said he was cold, scratched up, had abandoned his vehicle, and had been running from the police, through the woods, for several hours. At first his conversation wasn't making a great deal of sense. Someone had "set him up" he began; the police tried to apprehend him, but he had gotten away; he was going to have to leave the area immediately because he was going to be accused of a crime he did not commit. What in the world was he talking about!? Questions began pouring out of me like water from a stream. What crime? When did it happen? Why was he running from the police if he did not commit the crime? What was he going to be accused of? Why did he have to leave the area? His responses were vague, elusive and not coherent. "Mom, a couple of months ago something terrible happened, something unplanned and something I would never have imagined, and is far too much to tell you right now. Just know that I have to go, and that I love you very much."

I tried to understand what he was saying, to reason with him, telling him repeatedly that if he didn't commit a crime then he should not be running, but should contact an attorney immediately, and turn himself in. My words were falling on ears that were not hearing what I was saying. He had obviously already made up his mind.

"Mom, please try to understand that I have to leave this area. I need time to be able to think. You and I both know that because of my past record I will not get a fair trial in this area. I have been set up. You have to believe me." I wept, and told him I loved him very much. I did not agree at all with what he was about to do, but he knew I would be praying for him, for God to keep him safe and give him the wisdom to quickly do the right thing and turn himself in. "Matt, please don't take a long time to decide to turn yourself in," I said, "and please, don't tell me where you're going, because when the police come here looking for you, I want to honestly be able to say I don't know where you are." That was the conversation I had with Matt almost two weeks earlier.

In Marion Stroud's book, *Dear God, It's Me and It's Urgent,* one of her contributing writers says, "No one can persuade another to change. Each of us guards a gate of change that can only be opened from the inside. We cannot open the gate of another's will, either by argument or by emotional appeal." How true that statement was for Matt. He had always been strong-willed and I had never been able to change his mind once he made it up.

Hours after Tom, Dorothy and the police left, I continued to sit, immovable, in the living room, unable to focus on whatever I had been doing before. Someone once said, "Sometimes we go in search of answers only to be faced with more questions." That was where I was tonight; searching for answers, only to be faced with too many questions.

My thoughts turned to the family who had lost the eighteen-year-old son in something as senseless as a home invasion robbery.

I prayed, "Lord, I cannot begin to imagine the pain of losing an eighteen-year-old. Nothing will ever fill the void in that family's life. Lord, please put your strong arms of love around them and continue to comfort them. Dear God, please don't let Matt be involved in this."

I rested my head on the back of the chair, closing my eyes and thinking about the last four months and asking myself if there was anything I might have seen or heard which would have even remotely hinted that Matt could possibly have been involved in something as serious as this.

I didn't have to think long or hard to remember for the past several months Matt had simply not been himself. Something had been weighing heavily on him, something he had not been able to shake off. I recalled a day when he was here at the house. He seemed depressed, distant and forlorn. I asked him what was wrong, and if he needed to talk. He looked away from me when he responded and said, "Mom, sometimes things happen so unexpectedly in life, things that we did not plan, nor foresee, things that we cannot change or undo, no matter how much we wish we could...." He stopped there, leaving his thoughts dangling in midair. I waited for him to say more, but when he didn't I agreed with him, and told him that life often takes many unexpected turns in the road. I asked him again if there was something that he wanted to talk about. His eyes were sad and he shook his head. I hugged him and said, "Matt, you know I love you and I'm here if you do need to talk about anything."

Julia came into the living room interrupting my thoughts and asked, "Mom, aren't you going to get ready for bed? It's getting late and you looked tired." "Not yet, Julia. I just want to sit here a while longer, to think and to pray." Long after Julia had gone to bed I continued to sit, to think, to pray, and to ask God why.

My thoughts went back to when Matt and my other four children were little. Where had we gone wrong? We raised them in a Christian home environment. We home schooled them for close to seven years. When Matt was going into the tenth grade I put all five of them back in public school, and got a part time job outside of the home for the first time in fifteen years. Edward and I were still married at that time but our marital issues had already begun. He was adamantly opposed to putting the children back in public school, and would not give my feelings any consideration. I felt my season for home schooling was over, and I knew the children needed more of an academic challenge than I was educationally qualified to offer them at that juncture. The children also wanted the opportunity to go back to public school. When Matt was seventeen Edward and I separated and subsequently divorced a couple of years later.

Almost immediately Matt had problems adjusting to the public school environment, including problems being bullied, which led to him trying to handle it himself and getting into fights. I made numerous trips to the principal's office until Matt was suspended in his senior year, and would therefore not be allowed to graduate. The school had zero tolerance for fights, no matter who started it. Usually when Matt got into a fight, my two younger sons, David and James, also got involved, and it became one big mess. My daughters, Joanna and Julia, on the other hand adjusted well to the public school environment. Since Matt had not been allowed to graduate he took the GED exam and passed. There was no question about his intelligence. He was very smart.

For Matt, fighting, drinking and getting into trouble escalated through his late teen years and into his early twenties. Close friends felt it was because of Edward's absence from our once unified Christian home, as well as his lack of involvement in the children's lives. Edward was a workaholic and before we separated he would sometimes be away from home for days at a time.

Like Matt, David and James had involvement in the juvenile criminal system, in their teen years, although brief for the two of them. David and James began to mature as their focus changed from the adolescent issues, to making something meaningful of their lives. David became a dad and got married, in that order. James got a full time job and began taking classes at our community college. I was delighted to see things beginning to take shape for them in a positive way. Matt, however, chose a totally different path, and no amount of talking, fussing, counseling, or praying seemed to change him or motivate him to want to change. He ignored the fact that he had been raised in a Christian home and taught to make wise choices. He became involved in a number of legal situations causing him to be arrested at least a half dozen times, sometimes for petty things, like getting drunk and getting into fights, and other times for much more serious issues, such as forging a check. To my great dismay, before Matt was twenty he had a felony on his record. He considered going into the military but with a GED and a felony, he would not be given priority.

There is no question that the passage from an adolescent to an adult is a rough journey, especially for African American males, without the benefit of their dads in the home. When we were raising our children I felt if we did a good job teaching them and giving them a solid Christian foundation then they would have to turn out fine, and they would make good choices. I was naïve to think that way.

By 2003, Joanna, my fourth child, was in college and enjoying living away from home. My fifth and youngest, Julia, was a typical teenager who spent endless hours talking on the phone about boys or with boys. James and Julia were the only two still living at home. Matt turned twenty-four that year and had not had any legal issues for about two years.

Sometime in early 2003, I had an especially vivid, haunting dream about Matt that troubled me greatly. In the dream he was running in the opposite direction from where I was standing. He ran toward the edge of a great precipice that had an incredibly steep drop. He didn't seem to see what I could see. I could see that if he kept running he was going to fall off that cliff and the results would be disastrous. I called out to him repeatedly, loudly, trying to warn him, "Matt, please stop." However, the louder I called out to him, the farther and faster he ran from me, although I was certain he heard me. Suddenly, in the dream, as he neared the edge of the cliff, a man stepped out from the shadows, grabbed Matt and held him tightly. Matt struggled with the man and tried to break free, but the man was stronger and kept holding him, until all struggle was gone, and a great peace came over Matt. I knew beyond a doubt that the man in the dream holding Matt was Jesus, who had come to save his life. I knew in my heart Matt was still involved in things he should not have been involved in, although what those things were, I did not specifically know. Matt was not listening to anyone's advice about making good choices. I continued to pray for him, to talk to him, and remind him God has a wonderful plan for each of our lives, if we will seek Him first in all things. Sin sometimes makes a subtle entrance into a person's life and before they realize it there is such a stronghold there that they are no longer able to make wise, Godly choices.

Hours after the police and detectives left my house I finally went to bed, tossing and turning most of the night and not sleeping well at all. The next morning as I was getting ready for work I noticed two telephone company trucks parked across the street. Instantly I remembered what Tom said the night before about the probability of our phones being wire tapped. In the next couple of days I was fairly certain that had happened because there was a tremendous amount of static and clicking on the phone each time we received an incoming call. It was terribly annoying knowing someone somewhere was listening to every phone call that came into our house. I made a point of telling most people who called that the phone line was probably bugged. Some people commented that they could hear the clicking.

Sometime in November, several weeks after the detectives and the SWAT team had been to my home, a subpoena for me to appear before a Grand Jury for a hearing was delivered to me by Detective Ellis. I asked him if I needed an attorney present when I came in for the Grand Jury hearing. He said no. After calling Matt's attorney and asking him if he thought I should bring an attorney with me, he said, "most definitely." I contacted Ms. O'Hara, an attorney from a well-known law group in our area, whom our family had used on a number of occasions in the past. Ms. O'Hara was a petite, fragile looking blonde who was anything but fragile in the courtroom. She represented me several years earlier in my divorce.

On the morning of the hearing I was extremely nervous. Mrs. O'Hara said there was no way to prepare for the questioning that would take place, since we didn't know the questions that would be asked. I simply needed to give honest responses.

When I arrived at the courthouse I was surprised to see Rick and Cathy. Rick was one of Matt's close friends and had grown up in our ethnically diverse, middle-class neighborhood. There were several other young people there whom I didn't know, but who knew Matt, and who were also subpoenaed. Rick hugged me and asked how I was doing. Looking into his clear blue eyes, I was troubled by the sadness that I saw. I got the distinct feeling he wanted to tell me something, but for some reason he was unable to do so. There was no opportunity to talk privately with him, or ask him what was troubling him. Cathy, Rick's girlfriend, was pregnant, close to her due date, and clearly not at all happy about having to be there.

Ms. O'Hara arrived shortly. I was the only one who had retained an attorney.

We all sat together talking quietly, speculating about what we might be asked. We knew the prosecuting attorney representing the state was going to try and put together the pieces of a puzzle, hoping each of us held some vital piece, which would be used to determine where Matt might be. We were all surprised that my sons, David and James, had not been subpoenaed. Also, Chris, another close friend of Matt's, had not been subpoenaed.

Truthfully, I was glad I did not know where Matt was. Many times during the day, every day, I thought of him, prayed for him, cried for him, and asked God for the hundredth time, "why?" Why was this happening? Why in the world was Matt's DNA recovered from the scene of a crime? I had to put him totally in God's most capable hands or the burden would have been too much to bear. I had to trust God that Matt would be fine and no harm would come to him. I was totally perplexed about why he had chosen not to turn himself in.

We began to be called into the Grand Jury room, one by one. After a while we noticed no one came out of the room through the door they entered. We concluded that everyone was being sent out through another door, so we had no opportunity to ask the other person what questions they were asked. Mrs. O'Hara and I were called last.

We entered the room where twelve strangers sat around a large table, with expressionless faces. After being sworn in I noticed Detectives Jefferson and Ellis standing in the corner, quietly observing. Moments later one of the two prosecuting attorneys began asking me questions. The recorder in the middle of the table was a silent reminder to choose my words carefully. My knees were shaking under the table. Ms. O'Hara and I sat almost shoulder to shoulder. One of the questions I was asked was if I thought Matt was either selling or using drugs. Ridiculous, I thought! "Of course not," was my response. "Matt doesn't even like taking medication for a headache. Why in the world would he be using or selling drugs?" After what seemed to be an endless barrage of questions we were excused, and asked to wait in the hallway. Ms. O'Hara said we would likely be called back in a few minutes. We were, and the questions resumed with them asking me some of the same questions I'd been asked a few minutes earlier, just worded differently.

As we finished and exited the building Mrs. O'Hara and I spoke again about how odd it was that David and James had not been subpoenaed. She said I did a good job, and my answers were consistent. I told her I was glad it was over. Little did I realize this was just the beginning of an extremely long, never-to-be forgotten, journey!

The Thanksgiving and Christmas holidays came and went quietly, uneventfully, as 2003 came to a close. My prayers for Matt remained the same; that he would soon turn himself in. I could not imagine what he was thinking that caused him to elude the police instead of turning himself in. He knew the right thing to do. In addition to our phone being wire tapped, I suspected we were also being watched.

Several weeks after the Grand Jury hearing we heard Cathy lost her baby. I could not begin to express how sad I felt for her and Rick.

Other newspaper articles continued to come out in our local newspaper regarding Matt and the death of the young eighteen-year-old male. I was angry that the newspaper was printing stories which seemed to presume Matt was guilty.

I had so many questions for Matt. Had he been there? If so, what happened that night? Were others involved? Was he involved in the lifestyle of selling or using drugs?

Friends and neighbors who had watched Matt grow up found the accusations against him hard to believe, in spite of the fact that the police said his DNA was recovered from the scene of the crime, and in spite of the fact that he had been in trouble with the police since he was about seventeen. He was a personable young man, charismatic, handsome, extremely intelligent, a leader, never a follower. Each day I hoped would be the day I would get a call from him saying, "Mom, I've turned myself into the police. This has all been a terrible misunderstanding. I can explain everything and answer everyone's questions." Sadly, that was not the case.

Then one night in February, hours after I had gone to bed, the unexpected ringing of the phone awakened me. Abruptly I sat upright in bed, fumbling in the dark room to pick up the phone. Simultaneously James picked up the phone from his bedroom. It was Lauren, Matt's girlfriend, sobbing. "Mrs. Smith, they got Matt." My heart sank when I heard her words. My first thought was Matt had been shot. "What has happened Lauren? Tell me what has happened to my son, please." "My brother just called and said they came for Matt." "Who came for Matt, Lauren, and has he been hurt?" "My brother said it was the U.S. Marshals. They broke down the door, came into the apartment and took Matt. He didn't resist arrest and they did not hurt him. They told my brother that Matt will be extradited back to your area within the next twenty-four hours." "And where was Matt, when they took him, Lauren?" "He was in New Jersey, Mrs. Smith. That's where my brother called me from." "And where are you, Lauren?" "I'm in Georgia at my grandparents' home. My grand dad is gravely ill." I was silent for a moment as James began asking Lauren questions. Matt was alive and had not been hurt! Praise God! I asked her at least three more times if she was certain he had not been hurt.

I thought of the ordeal ahead for Matt. Our area has a long standing reputation for being hard on crime, and disproportionately excessive in the sentencing of minorities, even for minor infractions of the law. The charges facing Matt were by no means a minor infraction of the law. I knew my son had at least three strikes against him; being African American, being charged with murder, and having a prior police record. The road ahead for Matt would be unlike any he had ever walked.

Lauren stayed on the phone for almost an hour. I told her I was pretty certain our phone was bugged, and she should probably expect a visit from the police to pick her up for questioning.

The next day when I returned home from work I received a call from Lauren's grandmother. The police had come for Lauren during the early morning hours, after she got off the phone with us. Lauren would also be brought back to for questioning. Lauren's grandmother asked if I would go see Lauren at the jail, since they had no family in our area. I told her I would certainly do that.

Within twenty-four hours Matt and Lauren were both extradited back. Matt was flown to a nearby city accompanied by Detectives Ellis and Jefferson. Matt later told me that on the evening he was arrested, he saw a truck driving back and forth several times outside of the place he was staying. He said he felt his time was up, and he didn't feel like running anymore. He said what he remembered most about the extradition, was the humiliation of being escorted through the airports, in shackles and a brightly colored jump suit, and seeing the wide eyed stares of small children.

To my great surprise when Lauren was extradited back she was not placed in the women's division of the county jail as I thought she would be, but rather in the *juvenile detention center*. It turned out Lauren was not twenty one or twenty two, as I had been led to believe, but was seventeen years old!

Matt was taken to the county jail, and held without bond, since he was obviously a flight risk, with numerous charges, the most grievous being murder.

Lauren called to tell me she was at the juvenile detention center, and she could only receive visits from parents or guardians. She said she was going to list me as a guardian so that I could come see her. Otherwise no one would be coming to see her. If I could help in some way, I wanted to be able to do that and pass along information to her mother and grandmother.

About a week after Matt was brought back I went to see him. It had been over four months since I'd seen him. He was much thinner than he had been in October. He had gotten a tattoo on one arm, from his wrist to his elbow, resembling red flames. I wanted to be able to talk freely to him. I had so many questions, but we both knew our conversations would be recorded and he was really not at liberty to speak freely.

While Matt was still on the run one of his close friends had retained an attorney for him. After Matt was extradited back he decided he wanted to retain a different attorney, and in addition he wanted to pay for an attorney for Lauren. He asked me to pay them with money he had in various places, as well as at our house. I agreed to do that.

Each time I questioned Matt about where the money came from, he would only say I shouldn't concern myself with where it came from. It was money he earned, he said. He gave me the names of three well-known local attorneys, two were to be retained for him and the third for Lauren. His case was scheduled to go to trial sometime during the summer of 2004.

The attorney whom we retained for Lauren was able to get her released almost immediately. She returned to her family in Georgia for a couple of months, but said she would come back before Matt's trial was scheduled to begin.

2

THE RED FOLDER AND FIFTY
THOUSAND DOLLARS

MAY, 2004

Julia routinely called me every day at work to let me know she was home from school, and we would chat briefly for a few minutes. Today, however, the call I received from her was anything but routine. "Mom," she began, with such alarm in her voice that I immediately knew this was not going to be our usual call, "there are a lot of police in our house with a search warrant. Please come home right away. They are looking through everything. They said it's alright for me to go to a neighbor's house while they are here. Okay, Mom?" "Julia, go down the street to Cheryl's house. I will be there in a few minutes. Everything is going to be fine." Immediately I went into my supervisor's office and told her I had an emergency at home and had to leave.

The trip home usually took twenty minutes. I made it in half the time. When I arrived police cars were parked in front of my house, my neighbors' houses, and in my driveway. It was a lovely spring day, and a few neighbors were outside, while others were arriving home from work. Needless to say they were quite curious about what was going on at my house. I was greeted at my front door by a detective, "Good evening, Mrs. Smith. Please come in." Downstairs there were detectives in every room, but especially under the stairwell where I had some of Joanna's and Matt's things. The downstairs floor was littered with boxes of books and old record albums, Christmas ornament boxes, a folding ladder, and Matt's luggage that James had gone to New Jersey and brought back after Matt's arrest by U.S. Marshals.

Upstairs there was a beehive of activity as well. Detectives were in every room, looking in everything. I walked down the hallway toward my bedroom, which was obviously the hot spot because there were at least four detectives in there. As I stood in the doorway of my bedroom one of the detectives was holding my red folder, which he had found among my files. He began flipping through the papers of the folder. I held my breath. I knew it was just a matter of a few minutes before they would have evidence, written in my own handwriting, documenting dates and amounts of everything Matt had asked me to do with the money he left here. In addition to paying the attorneys that Matt asked me to retain, he had also asked me to give David money for payment of his outrageously expensive phone bill, courtesy of Matt calling collect from the jail, sometimes several times a day. "Good evening Mrs. Smith. Please have a seat in the living room for a few minutes," was the greeting I received from one of the detectives in my bedroom.

Taking a seat in the living room I picked up the newspaper and began turning pages, not actually seeing or reading anything. I tried to ignore everything that was going on around me. My thoughts abruptly turned to the previous day when James was outside cutting our grass and Matt called from the jail. Matt asked me to three-way the call to one of his attorneys. While I was on the phone with Matt and his attorney, James stopped cutting the grass and asked me to come outside. He wanted me to see the helicopter that kept circling directly over our house. He said someone seemed to be taking pictures of our house.

It was so blatant that a neighbor sitting on her porch walked over to us and said, "Wow, isn't that weird? That helicopter keeps circling over your house, as if they are taking pictures of your property." I told Matt and his attorney. Matt's attorney said, "Why in the world would someone in a helicopter be taking pictures of your house, Mrs. Smith?" "Yeah," I said, "You're right. Why would someone be taking pictures of my house?" As I sat on the sofa, flipping absentmindedly through the newspaper, I felt there was a definite connection between the helicopter circling over our house the previous day, and what was happening inside my house.

My thoughts came to an abrupt halt when I heard Detective Ellis ask for the folding ladder to be brought up from the downstairs. This time I could feel a large lump rising up in my throat. I mentally told myself not to panic. I knew exactly what they were looking for and what he was going to do with the ladder. Take deep breaths I told myself. Control your breathing. The ladder was placed in the hallway, directly under the opening of the attic. When I heard the attic open I think I stopped breathing for a few seconds. In less than a minute Detective Ellis re-emerged from the attic with a shoe box in his hands. "Bingo," he said, as all the detectives gathered around him to see what had been found. I continued to focus on the newspaper. There was $50,000 in that shoe box which belonged to Matt. The detectives talked quietly amongst themselves for a few minutes. I continued to pretend to ignore them.

Moments later James walked into the house from work. One of the detectives announced to James that they had just found what appeared to be a substantial amount of cash in our attic. James was surprised that money was in our attic, and rightly so, since I hadn't told him where Matt's money was hidden. Detective Jefferson asked me to come sit on the porch with him for a few minutes and talk. I groaned, put the newspaper down, and reluctantly went out on the porch with him. He tried to get me to talk saying he was not recording the conversation, but I refused to say anything. He finally gave up, clearly annoyed with me, and we walked back into the house.

When they were satisfied that all the money hidden in the house had been found, they got ready to leave, but not before announcing to James and me that we were soon going to be arrested. In fact, they said, probably our entire household, including David and Joanna, but not Julia. Joanna was away at college. I quickly, silently prayed our arrests would not be that evening and we would have some time to prepare. I asked them when would they arrest us and what would be the charges. The detectives said they didn't know what the charges would be, but as soon as the warrants were prepared in the next couple of days, we would be arrested. I asked if they would let me know when the warrants were prepared and I would turn myself in. They said they would do that. Unquestionably, even then, I saw the mercy and favor of God, since we were not arrested that evening.

When the police and detectives left, I crumbled into a chair and wept long, hot, bitter, tears. What in the world had I potentially put myself and my family in the middle of by trying to be there for Matt and help him? I had given my son the benefit of the doubt, and certainly believed he was innocent until proven guilty. However, by having the money hidden in my house and using the money he'd left in various other places, money that was definitely questionable, to pay attorney's fees, and various other things he'd ask me to take care of, I had potentially put all of us in a huge legal mess. Many times when Matt called, we would three-way the calls to each other so we could all talk to him at the same time. From a legal standpoint, that might constitute a charge of conspiracy.

The Word of God speaks in Luke 14:28 about how we should count the cost before we do anything. I had not even considered the cost to myself and to my family. How naïve and foolish I had been. I prayed that God would forgive me, show us His mercy, His undeserved favor, and protect us.

After the police left I called my attorney's office leaving an urgent message on their machine that I needed to get in to see her the very next day.

The next morning, before I left for work, I received a call back from Ms. O'Hara's secretary, Allison. "What's going on Mrs. Smith? Your call said it was urgent." I gave Allison a brief rundown of what happened the evening before; telling her of the $50,000 taken from the attic in my house, by the detectives, and that I had been told we were all going to be arrested when warrants were cut. Allison said Ms. O'Hara had court cases all day, and a packed schedule for the next couple of days, but she would squeeze me in, if I didn't mind coming after five that evening, and if I didn't mind waiting. I thanked her profusely and said I would be there, and certainly did not mind waiting.

When I got to work that morning I immediately went into my supervisor's office before other employees arrived and told her what happened. She hugged me and said I had put myself and my family in a terrible position of compromise, in order to help Matt. She shook her head saying, "Diana, you know I will pray for you. I truly hope this is all just talk from the detectives and you will not be arrested. After all, you have no criminal record of any kind and you held a top secret security clearance when you were in the military. Certainly that should count for something. You are one of the most honest and compassionate people I have ever known. But, Diana, you know that whenever we compromise ourselves and our integrity, for whatever reason, there is a cost involved. I will pray that God is merciful to you and your family."

At lunch time I met my friend Debbie, and we did our usual walk through the downtown area. I told her what happened the previous evening. She, like my supervisor, said she didn't think I'd be arrested. "What have you done wrong, Diana? Nothing! Paying attorneys with money that Matt left is not a crime. You do not know where that money came from. Matt did not give you a satisfactory answer to that question when you asked him. We can speculate about where it came from, but we have no proof or factual knowledge about how Matt obtained that money." I agreed. Before we went back to our respective jobs Debbie reminded me that if I needed help with Julia or anything, she would be available. I appreciated her friendship more than she could ever know.

After work I went straight to Ms. O'Hara's office. There were several people ahead of me. I sat nervously awaiting my turn, and once again absent mindedly flipped through the newspaper, as I had done the previous evening. My mind was in fast forward thinking about dozens of details which needed to be taken care of immediately, in the event I would actually be arrested. Mentally I made a list of everyone I needed to talk to, beginning with each of my children, then my church family, biological family, neighbors whom we had known for two decades, close friends, and Edward. I thought about all the "what ifs." "What if I really am arrested? What if Julia is left alone? Who will take care of her for me? She was almost sixteen, but she had never been away from me, except to spend the night with friends. What will we do? How will my bills get paid, especially my mortgage? I knew, even before talking to my attorney, that it was imperative that I name someone as a Power of Attorney person for myself, to take care of Julia and all the other things that would need to be taken care of, in the event I was actually arrested. There were at least a dozen people I could have asked, but I felt Sarah would be the best choice, for a number of reasons. She was a friend, whom I had known longer than any-one else in the area. She was also a born again Christian. She was wise and objective, and always a "no nonsense, get the job done" kind of person.

Allison brought my thoughts to a halt with, "Diana, Ms. O'Hara is ready to see you now." I went into Mrs. O'Hara's of-fice thanking her for seeing me on such short notice. We chatted briefly, and I began telling her what happened the day before at my house. She listened carefully, intently, taking notes, and inter-rupting only to ask pertinent questions. When I finished speak-ing she said, "What a mess Matt has put you and your family in the middle of by asking you to do those things for him. Diana, you are certainly a mother, and mothers often think with their hearts, not their heads. It isn't easy to be logical and objective when you love your children, and want to believe them. In all honestly, Diana, I think my mother would have done the same thing for me that you did for your son had she been in your posi-tion, without realizing the position she would have been putting herself in." I wiped tears from my eyes, and nodded my head in agreement. I asked her if she would be willing to represent me. She said she would be happy to.

Within the next twenty four hours I spoke to Sarah who agreed to be my Power of Attorney person. I spoke with my pastor's wife. I called family members, close friends, neighbors and Edward, who was furious with Matt, and certainly annoyed with me for the position I had put myself in by agreeing to help Matt.

I called my son, David and Beatrice, his wife. We went for a long drive in the country as I told them what had happened. Beatrice was extremely upset, but David's face was expressionless as he drove. When we got back to town they both hugged me and David said, "Mom, I love you. It's going to be okay. Please don't worry."

Bothering Joanna at college was not something I wanted to do, but I knew it had to be done, especially since she was also at risk for being arrested, since she was a part of one of those group phone calls with Matt. I called her and asked her to come home after her last class. I told her it was urgent and not something I could discuss on the phone. She came right away. We drove to a quiet place away from home, and talked and cried together. I told her I was probably going to be arrested, and there was a possibility the detectives might charge her with something. She had worked hard this school year, pulling her grades up, so she could be a part of the study abroad program. She was scheduled to leave the country in two weeks, and would be gone for more than six months. I prayed fervently that nothing would interfere. I asked the Lord to be gracious to her and protect her from whatever I was about to go through. I specifically prayed she would not be charged or involved in this situation in any way legally. I asked my pastor's wife and other Christian friends whom I knew were prayer warriors, to please double their prayers for Joanna to not be detained in any way. God heard and honored those prayers for Joanna.

Another close and dear friend, Madeline, whom I have known for more than two decades, drove over two hours from her home to see me. We left my house, drove to a restaurant and sat in the parking lot talking about what had happened. Madeline was greatly saddened by all of it, but especially by the decision I had made to help Matt, and the price she felt I was about to pay. She promised she would pray for us, and would be there as my friend, no matter what.

Two weeks later, in mid-May, we said goodbye to Joanna as she left for her trip abroad, without any problems whatsoever from the detectives. She was not scheduled to return to the United States until late December. I was immensely thankful to God for what I felt was a miracle. Before Joanna left I repeatedly told her that no matter what happened with us while she was away, she was not to worry about us, and she was not to come back home before her study abroad time was completed. I told her to focus on her studies to the best of her ability, and know that Julia would be taken care of, and we would be fine. I spoke by faith, because truly I did not know what the outcome of the situation would be for me, James, and David or any of us. I prayed much for God's favor for all of us. God would take care of us. I knew that much, because I know God, and I know He is a faithful Father, Friend, Deliverer and so much more. I reminded Joanna a number of times to, "just pray, and trust God for the outcome for all of us."

I talked to Julia every day to help her understand what was likely going to happen to me, James and David. She said she understood, but truthfully, none of us understood what was about to happen, and the impact it would have on our family and others for the rest of our lives.

Two weeks after Joanna left the country there was an uneasy quietness, like the calm before a great storm. Each day I woke up thinking perhaps that would be the day the warrants were issued and we would be called to turn ourselves in, but there was only silence. Each morning I hugged Julia an extra hug, and told her how much I loved her, before she went to school and I went to work.

On Friday morning Mrs. O'Hara called to tell me she was going out of town for the long Memorial Day weekend, and would return on Tuesday. She had spoken with the detectives during the week and they promised her, as they had promised me, that when the warrants were issued, they would call her and she would call me. Then David, James and I would go turn ourselves in. That was the plan, but that was not to be the case.

3

THREE ARRESTS

By lunchtime on Friday afternoon of the Memorial Day weekend, most of the staff at work had left for the much anticipated, long, holiday weekend. I stayed to clear up paperwork and to make a few calls. Earlier I had gone for my usual lunch time walk, but today I decided to walk alone. I always found walking to be a tremendous stress reliever as well as a time to sort out my thoughts and talk to God. Today I could have walked a hundred miles and it would not have lowered the level of stress I was feeling. Maybe I was stressing unnecessarily. Maybe everyone was right and we weren't going to be arrested after all. I was looking forward to the upcoming three day weekend.

At a little past 2:30 p.m. I picked up the phone to make a call, but before I could dial I heard someone in the hallway asking the receptionist, "Is there a Diana Smith in this office?" Seconds later two male police officers and one female officer walked into my office. "Are you Diana Smith" one of them asked? "Yes, I am," I responded, as I put the phone down. "Mrs. Smith, you are under arrest," one of them announced. "We were told that you are not to make any phone calls, and you are not to tell anyone you are being arrested." I quickly thought about Julia as I glanced at the wall clock opposite my desk. She would be getting off the school bus in less than fifteen minutes and she would make her usual phone call to me. I looked at the female officer and addressed my question directly to her. "My daughter will be getting off the school bus in just a few minutes. May I call a friend to go meet her and let her know?" The female officer answered without hesitating. "Yes, certainly." Quickly I dialed Debbie's office number and prayed silently, urgently, "Lord, please let Debbie be at her desk, and answer her phone." She answered. "Debbie, I'm going to need you go meet Julia today. I…I…won't be able to talk to her when she calls me. I won't be here." "Diana, are you being arrested?" "Yes, Debbie. That's correct," I replied. "Are they in your office?" "Yes, Debbie," I replied, choking back the tears. "Thanks so much. Tell Julia I love her. I've got to go now." The tears suddenly felt like a football stuck in my throat.

The officers were kind to me. They did not handcuff me, and they asked if I wanted to go down a back stairway or take the elevator. I chose a back stairway. The three officers and I walked out past the receptionist, who sat staring in total bewilderment. I did not stop to give her an explanation. When we got outside, in the back parking lot, I was then handcuffed and placed in the back seat of the female officer's cruiser.

As we headed to the Magistrate's office I asked the officer about David and James. She said another officer had been dispatched to go to James' job and arrest him. My heart sank. She told me David was on his way back from a job, in another city, heading home and he was contacted, via his cell phone, and told to go straight to the magistrate's office and turn himself in. Words could not begin to describe the pain I felt for my sons. This was really happening to us. I thanked God again, silently, that Joanna was out of the country and would not be arrested, and Julia would be taken care of.

As the officer made her way through the heavy Friday afternoon, pre-holiday traffic, I hoped no one that I knew would see or recognize me. I was certain the magistrate would release all three of us on a personal recognizance, also called a "PR release." I continued to fight back the tears. This was not the time for me to be weepy. This wasn't going to take long I told myself. As soon as we could talk to the magistrate we would be released. I was convinced of that.

We arrived at the magistrate's office and nothing went as I thought it would. After speaking with him for a few minutes and telling him I had never been in any kind of trouble and had no previous record, not even an outstanding traffic ticket, and that I was a single parent of a fifteen-year old, he looked sympathetic, and made a brief phone call, I suspect, to the office of the prosecuting attorney. He hung up the phone, scratching his head, and looking utterly perplexed. "Mrs. Smith, unfortunately I am not going to be able to release you. I certainly don't understand this, nor do I agree with what I have been told to do, given the fact that you have no previous record, and you are certainly not a flight risk. However, I have been given strict instructions to hold you. I fully expect you will be released on Tuesday, when court is again in session." I was in shock. That would mean being in jail the entire Memorial Day weekend. Unbelievable! He excused me from his office and asked me to take a seat in the waiting area. The female officer stayed in his office a few minutes longer and then came out shaking her head. "This just doesn't make sense to us," she said.

James arrived shortly, in handcuffs, escorted by a male officer. I hoped and prayed that James and David would most certainly be released. However, a few minutes later James emerged from the magistrate's office looking pretty much like I felt, having received the same response that I had gotten. The female officer and I headed back to her cruiser. This time I was taken to another location, finger printed and photographed. James followed us in the police car he was being transported in, and came in while I was being fingerprinted. We looked directly at each other and I asked him if he was okay. He nodded his head yes, without saying anything, even though I knew he was not. He asked me the same question and I also nodded yes. We both lied. I knew we were not okay. This was all surreal. We hadn't seen David yet. The words that God spoke in Exodus 3:12 briefly came to my mind, "I will be with you."

After the finger printing and photographing I was taken to the county jail, to be processed in. The female officer who had been with me for the past two hours said, "Mrs. Smith, I certainly wish you the best. I'm sure you'll be out of here on Tuesday morning when court is back in session." She released me into the custody of the intake officer at the jail, and the not so pleasant looking sergeant sitting behind the desk. I thanked her, and once again, tried desperately to hold back the tears. As the heavy steel door closed behind her, I realized how helpless and vulnerable I felt in this room full of uniformed officers, and other people being formally arrested and processed into the jail.

As I was being processed in, I thought of David and James. David was a hard worker, a good husband, and a wonderful dad. His children were five and three years old. James worked a full time job while attending college and was one semester away from getting his Associates Degree. Considering that both he and David had dropped out of high school a few years earlier, a tremendous amount of maturing had taken place in both of them.

I thought of my daughters. Was Julia alright? Had Debbie taken her to Sarah's house? How was Julia handling this? Joanna was an entire continent away and it would likely be a couple of days before she would know we had been arrested. Maybe we would be home before she got an email from someone telling her of our arrests. I didn't want her to worry. I had given her strict instructions that no matter what happened, no matter what news she received about us, that she should just pray, and stay focused on her purpose for being abroad, which was to study and further her education.

My thoughts were placed on hold for a moment as James was escorted into the intake room. This time as our eyes met I saw such sadness in his eyes that I almost wept. Minutes later David came in. David looked like his thoughts were a million miles away. He didn't seem to be focused on what was going on around him, although he was responding to the questions being asked of him. He appeared to be deep in thought, elsewhere.

I happened to turn and look down a long corridor. Suddenly I saw Matt being escorted by an officer and coming toward us. He was talking to the officer and not particularly noticing the people in the intake area. As he got closer I began to wave to him. He stopped talking, thrust his head forward and stared in disbelief until he stood directly in front of me. We stood face to face for a moment and hugged each other. "Mom, are you all right?" "Yes, I'm fine," I said. He turned and saw David and James, and asked what we had been charged with. As I held out my paperwork to show him the charges, a young officer behind the desk began to yell, and ordered me to step away from Matt, and step inside one of the temporary holding cells. I was ordered to have no further communication with Matt about the charges. Matt turned his back to me and faced the desk. He dropped his head and his shoulders began to shake. I knew he was crying. I called out to him from my cell. "Matt, I'm alright, and we're going to be fine. Please, just pray." I spoke by faith and certainly not based on how I was feeling at that moment. I knew Matt had been brought to the intake section for two reasons. The first reason was so he could see his family being put in jail, and the second was so he could also be served with paperwork for the same charges that David, James and I had been charged with. Those charges were, "Conspiracy, and conspiracy to commit money laundering." My attorney would explain exactly what those charges meant when I saw her on Tuesday.

Turning around in the holding cell I realized there was an extremely drunk female in the cell with me, talking to herself and complaining about something, with no audience except me. She said she was hungry, although she held a brown paper bag lunch with two sandwiches, a piece of fruit, and a drink, which the jail had given to her. She hadn't taken a bite of anything. I focused for a moment on her. I sat down on the bench next to her and encouraged her to eat something. I told her she would feel better if she ate. For a brief moment I prayed silently and determined in my heart if I had to be in this place, jail, then as of right now, as of this moment, "Lord, please somehow use me, and help me to take my eyes off of my own misery, hurt, pain, and humiliation. Help me to help someone else who is hurting." I knew this place could easily be an opportunity to whine, complain, and feel sorry for myself, or it could be an opportunity to witness for Christ. "Lord, please forgive me whatever I have done that was not right in your sight, and in the eyes of the law. Father, please, give me the courage and the strength I will need in this place, and help me to somehow be used by you and for you, for the time I am here."

I watched as Matt was served paperwork and then returned to wherever in the building they had brought him from. Paperwork was completed for David and James and they were each escorted out of the intake section and into some unknown part of the jail. My heart ached for each of my children.

I was called out of the holding cell and instructed to follow a female officer. I was given a blue plastic tote containing two woolen Army blankets, two sheets, two one piece khaki colored jumpsuits, two white towels, two pair of white, cotton panties, no bra, some basic hygiene items, and no washcloths. I was ordered to strip, and give everything to the wardrobe lady, including the black under wire bra I was wearing. No black bras were allowed, and especially no under wire bra. I was given a bar of soap and some mandatory delouse shampoo and told to step into the shower and use the delouse shampoo. When I protested about the delouse shampoo and told the officer I did not have lice, I was told every inmate coming into the jail is required to use the delouse shampoo. The female officer gave me the items and walked away. Momentarily I considered pouring the delouse shampoo down the drain. I don't have lice, and she isn't even watching me, I thought. However, I decided whether or not I was being watched, I would do what I was asked to do. So, I used it. When I first came into the intake section I surrendered my purse, watch, and jewelry. Now it was my clothing, right down to my underwear. I felt a part of my identity was being involuntarily surrendered that day. I suddenly had a new empathy for people who go to jail.

When I finished showering I was escorted to another holding area adjacent to the main population of the women's pod. I was told there were a number of men's pods or housing areas in the jail. However, there was only one section that housed the women. New inmates were not put into the main population with other women until after going to court, at which time it would be determined if the person was going to be released or held. On Tuesday I would go into court, meet my attorney there, and request to be released. Tuesday could not come fast enough for me.

Isaiah 26:3 (paraphrase) says the Lord will keep in perfect peace those whose minds are stayed upon Him. I knew God's Word, but it was difficult to keep my mind stayed upon Him at a time like this.

4

"GUESTS" OF THE JAIL

Hours after I had been formally arrested I was finally allowed to make several phone calls. I spoke to Julia that evening at Sarah's house and reassured her that we would most likely be home on Tuesday after court.

After being taken to a cell in the women's holding area my cell-mate was a woman named Hattie. Hattie freely admitted she was addicted to drugs, and sometimes became violent when she used. She said she had been in jail many times. She was at least ten years younger than I, but had no front teeth, and looked much older. She said I looked much younger than fifty-four years old.

It was quite an adjustment to share such a confined space with a female I did not know. I was nervous but Hattie and I got along fine. Our toilet and a small sink were in the cell with us. I was shocked to see that the toilet had no partition around it to separate it from our bunk beds, or to give us any degree of privacy when we each had to use it. I decided I would take one of the two sheets I had been issued and I would drape myself with the sheet whenever I used the toilet. It gave both of us some small measure of privacy. Hattie began to do the same.

For the entire Memorial Day weekend I had no appetite, but I made myself drink lots of water from the small sink in our cell, and I drank the four ounce container of milk which we were given with breakfast. Hattie educated me quickly and told me if the officers noticed I wasn't eating, they might send me to medical and I could be put on suicide watch. I simply couldn't bring myself to eat the food. It was unappetizing. The foods on the trays were basically empty starches, breakfast, lunch and dinner. There was little fresh fruit, no whole wheat bread or whole grain cereals, and no fresh or raw vegetables. Hattie said it was normal to have white rice, white bread, and white cake on the tray, with a small amount of an overly cooked vegetable, and perhaps four ounces of a tasteless turkey patty that resembled shoe leather.

I thought of my three sons and the other men, who generally have larger appetites than women, and wondered if they were given such meager portions of food, poor in nutritional value, and conducive to helping one quickly become a diabetic. Hattie said inmates complained all the time about the quality and quantity of the food, but in the numerous times that she had been a "guest" at the jail the complaints were ignored and nothing was ever done. Hattie was extremely thin, but had a voracious appetite. At my request she helped me by eating the food on my tray, as well as hers. She was delighted to have the extra food. I decided I would fast for the next couple of days and just have the liquids. I didn't want the guards to see any food remaining on my tray.

The weekend passed much too slowly, as I anxiously waited for court to be in session on Tuesday morning. I fully expected David and James's attorneys to also be in court on Tuesday morning to request their release. I prayed for favor for all of us.

At 4:30 a.m. on Tuesday morning I was awakened by the female duty officer, ordered to get dressed, and come into the dayroom area to be transported along with a dozen or so other females, who were scheduled for various court jurisdictions in our area that morning. By 5:30 a.m., we were removed from the pod and taken to a holding area to be transported. We were served breakfast as we waited. I had an opportunity to pray over the horrible food. I asked the women if they had any objections to me praying. No one objected. I told them I would also like to pray for God's favor to be on each of them as they went into the courtrooms. They were delighted to have someone pray for them for favor in the courtroom. We all bowed our heads as I prayed.

While we were being transported in the jail's van I realized I had not been outside or had any sunlight in four days. For a person who walks every day that is torture! My thoughts focused on what lay ahead for me, David, and James at our bond hearing shortly. I expected my attorney would be back from her long Memorial Day weekend, and we would either be bonded out, or released on personal recognizance. This would all be cleared up shortly I told myself and we would return to work and go about our daily routines until Matt's trial began and he would be found innocent.

As we arrived at the Circuit Court we were unloaded and shackled at the wrists, waist, ankles, and then to each other. The shackles cut into my ankles since I wasn't wearing socks. We were taken to a holding area in the building, close to the courtroom where our cases would be heard. We waited and talked quietly amongst ourselves. Periodically someone's attorney would come back into the holding area to speak to their client, and the holding area began emptying out as cases were called.

To my surprise it was not Ms. O'Hara who came back into the holding area to see me but Mr. Caldwell, another attorney from their law firm. Mr. Caldwell said Ms. O'Hara was still out of town, but had been briefed about my arrest over the Memorial Day weekend, and she would be returning within the next twenty four hours.

He said she was livid with the detectives, and the two prosecuting attorneys for their deception because they had lied about giving notification to us so we could turn ourselves in. Mr. Caldwell said the prosecutors had gone about this process of arresting us in a totally unnecessary, humiliating, and embarrassing manner. I wholeheartedly agreed and was fine with having Mr. Caldwell until Ms. O'Hara got back into town. All of the attorneys in their law firm were known to be excellent attorneys. Mr. Caldwell returned to the courtroom to wait for my case to be called.

There was an extremely quiet female in the holding area that morning. I noticed she was limping. She and I were the last two women waiting for our names to be called. We began to talk. Her name was Bridget. She had been charged with shoplifting, and in the course of trying to get away she had fallen and sustained a broken ankle. When she asked my charges I simply handed her my paperwork. She let out a low whistle after reading the charges. She told me she hoped I would get to go home that day, but in the event I did not get to go home, I should be careful whom I shared the details of my case with. She said sometimes the prosecutor "plants" someone in the pod as an informant, and the information will later be used against the person in court. I had no reason to doubt her, having already had a firsthand glimpse of their tactics. I took her advice seriously and listened carefully.

Bridget and I continued talking until our conversation was interrupted by the bailiff. "Diana Smith, courtroom," he announced, as he unlocked the holding cell to escort me into the courtroom. I nervously entered the courtroom and quickly glanced around to see both of my pastors sitting in back of the courtroom, as well as my prayer group's leaders, and a number of close friends. Their faces were filled with concern. Seeing my pastors in the courtroom was like seeing my family in the courtroom. I wanted to hug all of them and thank them for being there, and yet I felt so ashamed, immensely humiliated, and embarrassed beyond words. Again I struggled to hold back the tears.

Seated directly behind me was a handsomely dressed man, whom I didn't know, but who clearly had an interest in our case. I later found out he was Matt's newest attorney from a large nearby city. Matt apparently released the two attorneys he'd asked me to retain for him, and had hired the gentleman I saw in court. But where were David and James, and their attorneys?!

Before there was time to ask Mr. Caldwell any questions I was told to stand, state my full name, complete address and birth date. After we sat back down, I managed to whisper to Mr. Caldwell to ask about David and James. He said they had been brought to court earlier that morning, their respective attorneys had been present, and both of them had been released. That was wonderful news! I expected the same for myself.

However, nothing went for me as we expected or hoped for. One of the prosecutors was allowed to speak before Mr. Caldwell. He asked the judge to continue to hold me, without any kind of bond, because I carried out all of Matt's requests in regards to the money, and paying whomever Matt asked me to pay. The judge listened to him intently. When it was Mr. Caldwell's turn to speak, the judge was terse in her comments and seemed to ignore everything Mr. Caldwell tried to convey. I was not allowed to speak at all. Mr. Caldwell pointed out several times that this was not a trial, but a bond hearing. He told the judge I had lived in the area and in the same house for almost two decades, was not a flight risk, nor a threat to society. He told her I had served in the military and at one time held at top secret security clearance. I had always been a law abiding citizen, had no criminal record of any kind, not even an outstanding traffic ticket. He pointed out that I was a single, divorced, working parent with a fifteen year old daughter, and no biological family in the area to care for her, and I worked for the largest private company in our area. He told her my pastors were in the courtroom, as well as others who had known me close to two decades, and any of them would happily give a character reference on my behalf. Periodically the judge glanced at me with a look of disdain, but nothing Mr. Caldwell said seemed to resonate with her. The prosecutors were allowed to speak several times.

Sadly, I could already see where this bond hearing was going. The judge wasn't remotely trying to be compassionate toward me, or hear anything Mr. Caldwell was saying on my behalf. It appeared that I, like Matt, had already been judged to be guilty. I heard the judge, as if I were in a fog, saying, "Bond denied. I remand you to the court, Mrs. Smith." Mr. Caldwell whispered to me, "Mrs. Smith, in my opinion, you have committed no crime whatsoever. It is not a crime to pay attorneys with money your son left at your home. You did not know where that money came from." I nodded my head, and then naively asked him, "What did she mean, 'I remand you to the court'?" "It means you will not be going home today, Mrs. Smith. However, we will do all we can to get you out of here as soon as possible. This is ridiculous! You do not deserve this, and you are being treated most unfairly. Ms. O'Hara will come to the jail to see you, as soon as she gets back into town." I felt the hand of the bailiff on my shoulder. "Mrs. Smith, let's go." I quickly stood up, thanked Mr. Caldwell, turned and nodded my head toward my pastors, while trying to manage a smile. I was thankful for my pastors and the friends who were there for moral support. However, it completely baffled me, Mr. Caldwell, and everyone else, as to why the judge allowed David and James to be bonded out but not me.

When I got back to the jail I was allowed to call home. James told me Matt had decided to release the two local attorneys whom he had asked me to retain for him, and who had been working on his case for over three months. He decided to hire a more prominent attorney from out of the area that someone in jail recommended to him. I did not think Matt made a wise decision in switching attorneys. His case was less than two weeks away from its scheduled starting date. His new attorney would not have adequate time to prepare, which would be a terrible disadvantage for Matt, unless the new attorney could request and receive a postponement.

When I got over the initial shock that I was obviously going to be the unwilling guest of the jail for somewhat longer than the Memorial Day weekend, I prayed that my attorney would somehow be able to circumvent the judge's order, and find another way to get me out. In the meantime, I realized I would need to do some serious adjusting mentally, emotionally, physically, and maybe even spiritually to the new surroundings.

I returned to the cell with Hattie for the remainder of the week. The Lord was ever so gracious to me. He knew that on the inside I felt like a small, frightened child in this new, unfamiliar environment.

Each day I felt more depressed. I continuously prayed asking the Lord to please, supernaturally intervene and get me out of this place. I am well aware that God does not always say 'yes' to every request that His children asks of Him. I have also known Him long enough to know that sometimes He allows us to go through the battle; sometimes He takes us over or around the battle; but He is ever present and faithful, and always there with us in the midst of the battle. A former pastor once said, "There have been some battles that I have engaged in on my own, and had it not been for the intervention of the Lord, I would have sorely lost those battles." I knew if the Lord did not intervene on our behalf we would sorely lose the battle.

I bombarded heaven with prayers, and myself with numerous unanswered questions. Father, I know you care about us, so why didn't you somehow stop Matt from being involved in this lifestyle that the police are saying he was a part of? I knew the answer before I asked the question. It is because God gives us the freedom to make our own choices, whether those choices benefit or harm us. He doesn't manipulate us like a puppeteer manipulates puppets. Sometimes our choices are terrible, irreversible, and horribly alter the course of our lives in a direction we can never change. I call those the "watershed" turns in our lives, because nothing will ever be the same again.

After a week of being kept in the holding area I was told by the duty officer one morning that it was time to go out into the main population. I didn't want to leave Hattie, who had been so kind to me. Hattie, who was streetwise and jail wise, gave me what I considered a crash course about what I could expect, once I walked out into the main population of women. She suggested I not discuss my case with the women or tell them anything that was not already public information, because you never know how what you say can and will be used against you. Hattie's advice was similar to Bridget's a few days earlier. Hattie told me to just be myself, but not to allow anyone to take advantage of me. I listened and took seriously everything she said.

I prayed and cried before I left Hattie. The cell was like a security blanket from the unknown. I begged the officer to let me stay in the holding area, which was also used as an isolation area, but the officer assured me, just as Hattie had, that I was going to be fine in main population, and if I had any problems, with anyone, I shouldn't hesitate to report to the officer on duty. Hattie told me she would see me in about ten days, when she came out of isolation.

I gathered up my blue tote and walked into the dayroom, feeling like a child stepping into a lion's den. Many of the women were watching TV, playing cards, reading, braiding each other's hair, or just talking to each other. As I stepped into that massive dayroom, I felt the Lord allowed me to see the women through His eyes. There was no need to fear. He was with me, and they were women just like me, just like Hattie. They were wives, girlfriends, mothers, sisters, daughters. Most of them were probably there because, like me, they had not exactly made the wisest choices. The peace of God reassured me and I was suddenly no longer afraid.

A voice in the cavernous room called out, "Mrs. Smith." A young woman named Gigi, who was a friend of Matt, came rushing over and hugged me. Bridget also saw me and came over to me. Gigi began to cry when she saw me. She said she had seen the newspaper articles regarding Matt's charges and our subsequent arrests. "Mrs. Smith, seeing you in here is like seeing my own mother in here. I can't imagine what this must be like for you. I'm so sorry you have to be here. I know this is breaking Matt's heart to know the prosecutors have stooped this low. You don't deserve this, and you don't belong in here. You don't even have your Bible with you, do you?" I shook my head and replied, "No, I don't." Gigi asked me if I had an undershirt, or socks because it really gets cold in that part of the building at night. I told her no, and that even my bra had been taken. Gigi immediately went to her cell and came back with her pillow case filled with things she felt I would need. She gave me her NIV Study Bible, a sports bra, socks, an undershirt, good shampoo, a writing tablet, and some healthy snacks, that she had ordered for herself from the canteen. After not eating much of anything for over a week, I was delighted to have a few healthy snacks. I thanked her profusely, and hugged her, through tears. Bridget told me to tell her if I needed anything, and if I had any problems with anyone to just let her know.

Gigi was a young, single mom in her early twenties. She was in jail for credit card fraud. She had allowed one of her friends to come through her checkout line at a popular retail store where she would ring up clothing and other merchandise, using a credit card that didn't belong to either of them. They got caught. Both were charged but her friend cooperated with the prosecuting attorney, was given a suspended sentence, and got out of jail. Gigi was now awaiting sentencing, and her attorney told her she would probably get at least a year. Gigi was angry about the unfairness of the sentencing, but said she was thanking God that her two children were not in foster care, but were being cared for by her mother, although it was a hardship for her mother.

In the meantime my attorney came back into town, and subsequently came to see me. She reiterated some of what Mr. Caldwell previously said to me; that she was livid with the two prosecutors, and the detectives for their deceptive tactics. She said she wanted to get me out of jail as soon as she could. She felt our arrests had been designed to get Matt's full and undivided attention. The police suspected there were others involved in the crime Matt had been charged with. She said the prosecutors now felt they had enough evidence to substantiate the fact that Matt was a drug dealer. They wanted him to co-operate with them, to tell them who else was involved, and exactly what happened on the night the eighteen-year old was killed, but Matt refused to say anything. Ms. O'Hara said David, James and I, in her opinion, were like pieces on the chess board being moved in an effort to get to Matt.

When I had been at the jail for about ten days I was taken to Medical. I was told it was routine for new inmates to go to Medical for a physical exam and weight check.   After they weighed me, I realized I had lost nine pounds in the ten days I had been there. Medical did not know the amount of weight I had lost because they did not weigh me on the day I was brought in, but I knew. I didn't tell anyone how much weight I had lost. I sat there thinking how long it had taken them to have me brought to Medical. I thought about people who have been living on the streets, and are sometimes ill or even contagious when they are brought in. If those people had to wait over a week, as I had to, and I wasn't even sick, that could be a serious problem for the people around them. Without a doubt it showed the jail's failure to prioritize and their lack of concern for the health of the people coming into the facility. It made more sense to me that people should be seen in Medical on day one, before they are brought to the holding area, and certainly before they are put into the main population with other inmates.

When I got back to the pod I randomly asked some of the women how soon they were taken to Medical for a physical after coming into the jail. All of them, without exception, said it had been well over a week, and in some cases longer.

Each day I told myself I was a temporary guest here who would hopefully be leaving shortly.

5

BOND STILL DENIED

After Hattie my cellmate was Naomi, a brunette, in her early thirties, with dark brown eyes and a wide smile. Naomi, like Hattie, was in for using drugs. She was a single mom with two children. Her elderly mom worked in a factory and took care of her children while she was incarcerated. Like Hattie, Naomi had been incarcerated several times previously, always for drug usage. Her biggest fear was she would get out and go right back to old habits and old friends. During the weeks that we were cellmates I prayed often for her to be strong when she got out, for her addictions to be broken, and that she would never again return to any jail.

Naomi was a tray server in the pod, and when she found out I didn't eat much of what was on the regular trays but generally passed my tray on to someone else, she made a habit of getting something off the extra diabetic trays for me to eat. The kitchen always sent extra diabetic trays that were trashed if no one ate them. Naomi knew I would eat any fresh fruit, or whole grain bread. Thankfully, I was not a diabetic, but the diabetic trays were much better, nutritionally, than the regular trays. I never asked her to do that, she simply did it. She would say, "Mrs. Smith, you are losing so much weight! You really need to eat more." After a while, whenever there was fresh fruit, which seemed to be just a couple times a week, I would sometimes get five or six apples from various different women, who would come over to me and say, "Mrs. Smith, I saved my fruit for you." They seemed to watch me like a mother hen watching her chicks. They would sometimes say to me, "Mrs. Smith, you haven't been eating. You didn't eat breakfast or lunch today. You are losing too much weight. You need to eat."

All the tray servers generally sat together to eat their meals, after they had served our trays. Naomi told me one day the women asked her what it was like to have me as a cellmate, because they usually saw me either reading the Bible or writing, when I came out into the dayroom. She said she told them it was like having an angel in the room. The day room was always a bee's hive of activity with the television on full volume and dozens of women talking at the same time. Naomi said sometimes she just needed to come back to our cell and get away from all the noise. She said as soon as she walked into our cell, it wasn't just a quiet place, but there was an indescribable peace always present. I knew it was the presence and peace of the Lord that she sensed in our cell, because I would generally pray out loud and talk to the Lord when she was out of the cell. God's peace is the kind that passes all human understanding and defies logic.

For weeks Ms. O'Hara tried unsuccessfully to get the judge's decision to not allow me to be bonded out, overturned. She took her argument to the State Court of Appeals in our state capital. Still it was denied. None of us understood why I continued to be held. Just because God seems to be silent doesn't mean He is absent.

In those first weeks when I spent time alone in the cell, I did my share of crying, whining, feeling sorry for myself, and begging the Lord to get me out. I repented of anything I did for Matt, which was not right in the eyes of God, or was legally wrong. I interceded in prayer for each of my children. I prayed for the mercy and favor of God over our lives. I prayed for anyone else who was involved in the crime Matt was said to have committed. I prayed for the women in the pod, and the officers who would work in the pod each day. From past experiences I knew the only way we were going to get over this mountain would be through much prayer and fasting.

I developed a routine and decided I was still going to get up early every morning, just as if I were home, and just as if I were getting ready for work. Each morning while my cellmate was still asleep, I would get up, take care of my hygiene, get dressed in my jail issued jumpsuit, and begin to pray softly so as not to disturb my cellmate. After prayer I would read the Word and meditate on the scriptures I had read. I knew many of the women stayed up half the night, talking, laughing, gossiping or playing cards. I came out of the cell each day for all meals even if I didn't eat anything on the tray. However, I kept myself well hydrated every day, refilling my eight-ounce plastic cup many times during the day with water. I was determined to trust God for the outcome of this horrendous situation and to have "mountain moving faith" instead of "light switch faith." I call "light switch faith" the kind where a person believes based on what they see, feel or think.

There were no windows in the women's pod so we never knew what the weather was like unless we were being transported to court. The women's recreation yard was a windowless room with a concrete floor, instead of an actual yard. The rec yard-room had a few pieces of outdated gym equipment and a basketball hoop.

Sometimes I would go into the room and exercise to relieve some of the stress. To get daily exercise one of the other women and I would speed walk in the pod, touching all four corners of the enormous day room. We would walk perhaps forty five minutes at least twice a day.

Prior to going to jail I naively thought only women who were "outcasts of society" went to jail; but when the shoe was on my foot, and I was suddenly there, I saw incarcerated women from a totally different prospective. As I got to briefly know some of the women, it became much more obvious that crime and bad decisions know no race or class of people. People of every color, social and economic status, make bad decisions and commit crimes that land them in jail. There was a nurse who was there for prescription fraud, and an accountant, who embezzled an incredible amount of money from a large firm that she worked for in our area. There was a grandma who ran over her two timing boyfriend with her car, as well as a doctor's daughter who had been arrested numerous times for drunk driving, and the college student who stole her roommate's credit card and maxed it out. There was the "expected group," the prostitutes and shoplifters. Then there was Lydia, a twenty-two-year-old single mother of two small children, who had been invited to New York with her new boyfriend on what he told her was a business trip for his job. He gave her money to shop while he went to his business meeting. On their way back home they were pulled over by a State Trooper because a tail light was out on the car. For some reason the trooper asked the young man to open the trunk of the car. To Lydia's surprise there was a large quantity of cocaine in the trunk. Lydia and the young man were both arrested, with both of them saying they knew nothing about the cocaine. Someone bonded him out, but the young woman's family could not afford to bond her out. She had been in jail for months, and had a court appointed attorney who was doing little for her. Her grandmother was caring for her children. Lydia was looking at getting several years if convicted. My heart hurt for Lydia and the dilemma she was in.

Some part of me felt like a wounded animal who wanted to retreat to a place where I could nurse my wounds, and feel sorry for myself. Some days when I prayed I did not *feel* like God was even in the room with me. He must be so disappointed in me. Hence the reason I was here. Wasn't I supposed to be a mature Christian? I had been a born again Christian for over two decades. Wasn't I supposed to be operating my life in a lot more wisdom than I had recently shown? Although I had all of these thoughts, I knew He was right there with me no matter how I felt, or what I was thinking, or read in the newspaper with regard to our case. My prayer continued to be "God, please, help me to walk by faith, not by sight or how I feel at the moment."

What matters is what God's Word says, even when life and circumstances bring bitter disappointment and sorrow, and when it seems God has removed Himself totally from the situation. God tells us in Hebrews 13:5, (NIV Bible) "Never will I leave you; never will I forsake you." Joshua 1:9 (New American Standard Bible) says, "For the Lord, your God, is with you wherever you go." That means even in jail. I decided I needed to interact with the women more, and not stay in the cell as much as I had been doing.

Each day I asked the Lord to tell me when to go out into the day room. I asked Him to help me to see and feel beyond my own painful situation, to see and feel the pain of other women and to offer them the only hope I knew, Jesus Christ. I prayed, "Lord, please allow me to be a good listener, to give wise counsel, and perhaps, in some way, to be a help and a blessing to those who do not know you as their Lord and Savior."

Sometimes my cellmate, Naomi and I would talk for hours at night as we lay on our bunk beds. We talked about growing up, about our families, our children, our dreams and hopes, and about some of the significant and insignificant men who had been a part of our lives. I told her how God loves us unconditionally, in spite of the messes we've made and in spite of how we have all fallen short. He is still the God of another chance, and we all need another chance. The mistakes we have made do not stop God from working in our lives; but because of poor choices, rebellion, and lack of faith we can certainly hinder what God desires to do.

Sometimes I would hear Naomi crying softly when our lights went out. Some nights I would sit on the floor, against the wall, and read scriptures to her. Her eyes would fill with tears. Naomi and I remained cellmates until her release. The night before she was released I prayed with her that she would never again come back to any jail. I prayed that Satan's hold on her through her drug addiction would be broken, by the blood, and the Name of Jesus Christ. That night Naomi gave her heart to Jesus and accepted Him as her Lord and Savior in that cell.

My church family continued to be wonderfully supportive, as well as a number of close friends and many of my neighbors. My church family prayed, fasted, interceded, sent money for canteen, visited, wrote letters of encouragement, came to court for us, made phone calls, accepted collect phone calls from me, cut the grass at my house, and kept Joanna abreast of what was happening with us, via phone calls, letters, emails and so much more. Words cannot begin to thank them adequately for all the tender loving care that was shown to us, and especially to Julia. This was not a mega church of thousands of people, or even hundreds of people, where resources seem to be endless, but this was a small, close knit, local community church of less than one hundred and fifty people. It is a church of strong, committed, dedicated, born again Christians who became the hands and feet of Christ for my family.

When I initially spoke to Sarah about not only being my Power of Attorney, but taking care of Julia, should we be arrested, she agreed. None of us anticipated that it would be for an extended period of time. Julia ended up staying with Sarah's family full time during the week, since David worked a full time job in addition to taking college classes. When it became obvious that I was not going to be getting out after the Memorial Day weekend, I asked Sarah if she would continue taking care of Julia. She agreed again. I told Sarah if, at any point, it became too much for her, she was to be honest with me and tell me, and I would make other arrangements for Julia. Sarah was a wife, a mother of two teenagers, worked a full time job for the federal government, and was extremely active in her church, among other things. I knew she already had much to keep her busy, in addition to taking on the added responsibilities for me. She agreed to help, and she agreed to let me know if it became a hardship to her, in any way. She has always been a wonderful friend.

Madeline, whom I have known for more than two decades, also went the extra mile for us. Madeline and her husband contributed toward the payment of my mortgage for the time I was incarcerated. Had it not been for them I very possibly would have lost my house of seventeen years. Edward continued contributing money each month, which Sarah used to pay the utilities, and cover other basic household expenses. God so graciously and mercifully provided. Madeline and her husband made it clear the money was a gift from them, and they did not wish repayment of it. She wrote long letters to me every week, with much needed words of encouragement and hope. Her letters reminded me of God's great and unconditional love for us. He is always merciful, even in His quiet moments, when we feel He isn't there, because maybe He isn't answering our prayers the way we'd like Him to.

God continuously sent encouragers to remind me to put my hope and trust in Him, because He does not disappoint His children. I needed a sustaining word from a sustaining God. Psalm 25:1, 2 says, "To you, O Lord, I lift up my soul; in you I trust, O my God. Do not let me be put to shame, nor let my enemies triumph over me." God's Word was the anchor for my soul, firm and secure.

In one of the letters Madeline wrote to me, she addressed it, "Diana Smith, Guest." My cellmate and I laughed for hours when I read that. It seemed I hadn't laughed in weeks. I started saying that to myself every day, "I am a guest here, an unwilling guest, but a guest nonetheless. I will be leaving soon." Even when I didn't know if I believed those words, I spoke them into my spirit, by faith. The Word of God says faith comes by hearing, and hearing by the Word of God. Madeline and her husband came one night to see me. They traveled over two and a half hours, during rush hour traffic, after working all day. I was delighted to see them. It was a wonderful, encouraging visit.

My dear friend Debbie was a treasure. She accepted my collect phone calls from the jail, updated me on things that had gone on during the week, in court, when Matt's trial was in session, and kept me posted on how Julia was doing. She read me the latest email from Joanna, and told me what was going on with David and James. David and James did not come to see me after they were bonded out. Perhaps it was too much for them to see me in jail. I understood.

Debbie always had a way of making me think about what she called, "the worst case scenario." One day during one of our phone conversations she told me I needed to think about the "what ifs" of this situation. What if I got sentenced to prison time, she said. I didn't like to think too long about the "what ifs" because some things were too overwhelming for me to focus on. I told her I had to continuously put all the "what ifs" into the most capable hands I knew of, the hands of my Father God, who sees everything and makes no mistakes. I had to trust Him no matter what happened. He would still be my Father, and I would still be His forgiven child. Before I was arrested it was necessary for me to focus on some of the "what ifs," the biggest one being, "what if I go to jail?!" That temporary focus had allowed me to prepare my children, as well as designate my Power of Attorney to take care of my personal affairs. But here, in jail, I had to take one day at a time, and every time a negative thought came to my mind, I prayed, gave it to God, and said, "Lord, God Almighty, I thank you for taking care of us, no matter where we are and no matter what our family is going through. Thank you also that no matter what the outcome of this situation, I will continue to trust you, and not lean on my own understanding. Lord, let me remember that nothing happens to us except first it has filtered through your wise and loving hands. You were not surprised by this situation and it did not catch you off guard. Me, yes, but You, no. As long as you are with me, and never leave me, I know it's going to be alright."

6

NO END IN SIGHT

When Naomi went home I was moved to the lower tier of the pod, and my cellmate was Christie. There were usually about fifty women on each tier. There was no special significance to being on either the upper or lower tier in the pod. It was simply where the duty officer chose to put you, or where there was an empty bed. On the day Naomi left the duty officer decided to move me to the lower tier.

One of the women on the lower tier said, "Oh, Mrs. Smith it's so nice to have you on this tier with us. It's our turn to share some of the anointing God has placed on you. We hear your prayers are powerful." I was so humbled by the comment and thankful because I knew it was Jesus in me that the women saw.

Christie was clearly not happy to have me as her new cellmate. She wanted her friend to share the cell, but the duty officer was not trying to put the two of them together. Christie was moody and grumpy all morning. I read my Bible, and stayed on my top bunk, unless I had to use the toilet. If Christie asked me a question I responded and continued reading. When it was our tier's turn to be out in the dayroom I stayed in the cell and continued reading, but Christie went into the dayroom. A couple of ladies stopped briefly at our cell door and asked how things were going with Christie. I said, "Well, she's made it pretty clear that she would rather not have me as her cellmate. Other than that we are fine." A few minutes later I saw Bridget pull Christie to the side and begin speaking to her about something. I'm not sure what Bridget said to her, but Christie came back into the cell and apologized. "Mrs. Smith, I didn't realize what has happened with your family, and why you are here. I'm really sorry I acted the way I did toward you. The women speak highly of you." I told her no problem. I understood.

About a week later three new females moved into the cell next to us. The first night they arrived they stayed awake until the early hours of the morning laughing, talking, and cussing, as if they were at a social function, instead of in jail. The duty officer for the night shift didn't seem to care and never once came to their cell to tell them to quiet down. Periodically, their loud hyena laughter would awaken me and probably everyone else around them. I covered my head, prayed and went back to sleep. Christie was furious with them. She banged on the wall several times and told them in no uncertain terms to tone it down, and cut out the cussing. They ignored her. The next morning as soon as the cell doors popped open for our tier to come out for breakfast, Christie practically flew out of our cell and headed directly to theirs. I said a silent prayer that she would be tactful and not get into a physical altercation with them. After all, there were three of them and one very petite Christie, who would be no match for them. Christie positioned her five feet, two inch frame in the entrance of their cell door, blocking the three of them from going out. She spoke loud and clear, telling them they were inconsiderate and extremely rude the previous night. She said, "I have a woman of God in my cell, and you are going to have to show some respect for her and the rest of us. I mean it. She shouldn't have had to listen to all the cussing ya'll were doing, and I don't want to have to speak to ya'll again about this. Do ya'll understand me?" Wow! I thought. What guts to confront three women, and all of them were bigger and taller than Christie. When they saw me at breakfast they each came over to the table and apologized. After that we had no more problems with them. Christie and I got along great for the short time we were cellmates. I was reminded that God always takes good care of me, and shows His great favor to me, no matter where I am.

A couple of weeks later I was moved back to the upper tier with a new cellmate, Patty. Some of the women said I got moved more than anyone else in the pod because I never complained. When some of the others were told to move they would fuss and complain so much, that sometimes the duty officer would just select someone else she knew wouldn't complain. That was me. I was never trying to give the officers a hard time or make their day any more difficult than it must already be for them in this environment.

In the weeks and months that followed, I remained in jail day after endless day not knowing when, or if, I would go home. I prayed like I had never prayed before. "Lord, why don't you get me out of here? I want and need to go home to take care of Julia. Please Lord, Julia needs me, and I certainly need to be there for her." No matter how much I prayed, it was as if the Lord had a different agenda for me, and going home was not on it at the moment.

In Max Lucado's book, *In the Grip of Grace,* he asks the question, "Is God still a good God even when He says no to us?" My response is absolutely! Yes, He is! I reminded myself constantly to not look at the circumstances, but to look to Jesus, no matter how things appeared to be in the natural realm. God allowed this to happen, and was well aware of everything happening to each one of us, moment by moment.

Matthew 10:29 and 30 (paraphrased) says, not even a tiny bird falls to the ground, except that God sees it. We brought the problem on ourselves, by the choices we each made. In II Samuel 24:14 King David says, "I am in deep distress. Let us fall into the hands of the Lord, for His mercy is great; but do not let me fall into the hands of men." My sentiments exactly.

Many times during the day, every day, I spoke God's word out loud, for myself, my children, and our monumental dilemma, because faith comes by hearing. I wrote out faith scriptures that comforted and encouraged me to keep my eyes and mind on God, and I meditated on God's words as if my life depended on it, because I knew it did.

Matt's girlfriend, Lauren, had been out of jail for months. Shortly before Matt's trial was to begin, she returned to our area to be present for his trial. She asked to stay at our house. I gave permission because I thought it would be good to have her there to encourage and motivate Julia. Although Julia stayed with Sarah's family during the week, she came home on weekends, when James did not have to work. Debbie and Sarah had reservations about having Lauren stay at my house. They felt Lauren was not an innocent bystander in Matt's case and might well have her hands in something illegal, like selling drugs, as the police were saying Matt had been doing. I couldn't imagine she would be doing that, given the fact that she knew the mess Matt was in. I gave her the benefit of the doubt allowing her to stay at my house. Sometime later I would find out just how wrong I had been.

One of the saddest days for me, at the jail, was Julia's sixteenth birthday. I wept sad, bitter tears all day because I could not be with her. Even my cellmate was sad and said, "That child should not have to bear the brunt of this mess, Mrs. Smith. It's a sad shame the judge won't give you a bond to be able to get out of this place. My heart breaks for Julia. I can only imagine what she has had to endure each day at school in this fish bowl of a town." That evening I called Julia at Sarah's house and wished her a happy birthday through teary eyes. Sarah and her family took Julia and James out to eat at Julia's favorite restaurant that evening. I was so appreciative of Sarah's thoughtfulness. Later in the week one of my neighbor's took her to the beach with their family. I thanked God for His blessings and His favor for Julia, and our family.

My cellmate, Patty, was a tiny blond who had been arrested because she and her boyfriend got caught with drugs in a hotel room. She had four children, including a set of twins. Every day she would take out pictures that her mom sent of her children, and begin crying. She said she had not had custody of any of her children for years. According to her she had been in every addiction treatment and rehab program in the state, but still returned to her old habits, and old friends after each treatment program ended. As I listened to her, I could only feel sympathy for her. She loved her lifestyle more than her children, and confessed she really had no intention to ever stop what she was doing, and would probably do drugs for the rest of her life.

Patty needed Jesus desperately. Each time I would begin to tell her about the Lord she was quick to tell me she was already a Christian. God's word says you will know His children by the fruit in their lives. I certainly saw no evidence in Patty's life or the lifestyle she had chosen, to suggest she had a relationship with the Lord Jesus Christ. I concluded that being a Christian for her was simply a title she used to distinguish herself from other religions. She had little knowledge of the Word of God, and had a horrible reputation in the pod as a liar, a thief, a con artist, and huge gossiper. Many of the women knew her from the numerous times she had been there.

Patty asked lots of questions about my case, much more than any previous cellmate. I remembered Bridget and Hattie's advice about not talking about my case, in detail, until it was finished. I especially did not wish to discuss it with Patty, the gossip columnist of the women's pod. When I answered her questions, I only gave her information that was common public knowledge, and had been written about in the newspapers, nothing beyond that. She could never brag that she knew some juicy tidbit of information that no one else was privy to. I never trusted her, and wondered if she could have been the prosecutor's "plant." Some of the other women in the pod must have had the same thought, because more than one of them said to me, on more than one occasion, "Mrs. Smith, do not trust Patty, and don't tell her your business. You never know what the prosecutor has up his sleeves." One day when I came back from court Patty was gone. We heard she had been moved to another jurisdiction.

One day a thin, wiry woman with a pleasant smile saw me sitting in the day room reading my Bible. Her name was Martha. She asked if I prayed for people. "Yes, of course," I said. Right away she sat down with me and asked if I would pray for her and her little son that her mother was taking care. Martha was an alcoholic. She said she became violent when she drank. She had made enemies with her child's father, with her current boyfriend, with her mother, and other family members, and no one was coming to see her or sending her money for canteen. I prayed with her and we started walking together daily in the pod. I talked much to her about our attitudes, and how we sometimes hurt the people who love us most. I talked to her about forgiveness, and about asking God and her family to forgive her for what she had done to hurt them. I even talked to her about getting professional help for the alcoholism, since she had never done that. At the same time I told her that all the rehab programs on the planet can never bring about the kind of lasting change which comes when we ask Jesus into our hearts and lives and begin to have a relationship with the Living God. She said she wanted that. I prayed with her to accept Jesus. We both wept.

When Martha and I walked we would use that time to pray for the officers on duty. We'd pray for better food trays. We'd pray about whatever the Lord put on our hearts to pray for. One day Martha specifically asked me to pray for her family to come see her and bring her little son. I helped her compose a letter to her family asking them to forgive her of the hurt she had caused them and telling them she now had Jesus in her heart and life. One night, about a week later, when it was visitation time, her name was called. She could hardly believe it. In all the months she'd been there no one had been to see her. One of her family members came that night and brought her little son. She was beside herself with joy when we all returned from visitation. She started gathering women in the pod that she felt needed prayer, or just needed someone to talk to. She would bring them to me, and say to them, "Talk to Mrs. Smith, and let her pray for you, and you will see what God can do."

We informally began having Bible study time and prayer group, sometimes in the middle of the day, and sometimes at night. We didn't plan it. It just happened. I would come out into the dayroom with my Bible, look for an empty table away from everyone else, and begin reading. Shortly, someone would come over to the table and ask a question or just sit down and begin talking. Within a few minutes we would have more women at the table than we had seats for. We talked about many things relating to the Gospel of Jesus Christ, but especially we spoke of the love of God. We talked about forgiveness, and not trying to get even with those who hurt you. We talked about trusting God for the outcome, no matter how badly things look, and how He disciplines those whom He loves (Hebrews 12:6). We talked about the "fruit of the spirit" being evident in the life of God's children, as spoken of in Galatians 5:22, "But the fruit of the Spirit is love, joy, peace, patience, kindness, goodness, faithfulness, gentleness and self-control." I told them that being a Christian does not mean you are perfect, but it does mean there is forgiveness and restoration when we confess our sins to God.

Our prayer group grew amazingly. Most of the women desperately wanted someone to pray with them and for them. Still, there were some women who never came near our prayer group and wanted nothing to do with it, and that was okay. We said a prayer for them as well. I knew God would send the ones whose hearts were ready to receive the Word of God. I began to encourage the women who expressed an interest, to ask for an NIV Study Bible since I felt it would be easy for them to understand. I encouraged them to begin reading in the New Testament as well as the Psalms and Proverbs. One day the pod officer was passing out mail for the day, and quite a few new Bibles arrived for some of the women. The officer said, "Gee whiz, I think we're handing out more Bibles today than mail." I was delighted to hear that.

My new cellmate said before I came only a few women had a Bible, and if they did they would not dare to bring it out into the dayroom, for fear of being made fun of. She said before I came, just a handful of women attended the Sunday afternoon church services. Most would stay in their cells and sleep all day. After I started encouraging the women to put in requests for Bibles, many started attending the mid-week Bible study, and many more began attending the Sunday afternoon church services. Church attendance grew and the request for Bibles continued on both tiers of the pod. Many of the churches in the area were kind enough to provide the Bibles.

One night so many women were in our prayer group who wanted prayer, that we formed a circle which just seemed to get bigger and bigger. The duty officer came rushing over when she saw such a large circle forming. She said she thought there was going to be a fight. We laughed and told her we had formed the circle to pray. She was clearly surprised and then quickly said she would allow all of us to go into the recreation yard room for a few minutes to pray so we didn't disturb the women who were watching TV and who did not want prayer. After that night none of the officers ever rushed over to see what we were doing when we came together to pray.

We prayed about many things, but we especially prayed for the children of the women, and for the caretakers of those precious children. We prayed for healing, restoration, new beginnings, and for addictions to be broken by the Blood of Jesus Christ. We prayed for favor in the courtrooms; for God to change hearts, and teach us how to walk in forgiveness and newness of life, in Christ Jesus and we always prayed for the pod officers.

It is easy to feel hopeless, helpless and powerless when a person is incarcerated. Some of the women never had visitors and rarely got mail, unless it was legal paperwork. I wanted them to know Him, and His incomprehensible love, acceptance and forgiveness for each one of us, no matter what we have done. Yes, there are consequences for our actions and for bad choices, but one of my favorite things to tell the women was, "God is the God of another chance, and the God who has a wonderful plan for our lives."

Jeremiah 29:11 (paraphrased) says, "For I know the plans that I have for you, plans to prosper you and not to harm you, plans to give you hope and a future, if you will call upon My Name."

One of the women in the pod was a beautiful African American woman with red hair and freckles. The women called her "Red." She was sociable, extremely talkative, and enjoyed being in the middle of whatever gossip and activity was going on in the day-room. I noticed though, when she saw us gathering for prayer or Bible study, she would stop whatever she was doing and come near to where we were. She would stay just on the outskirts of our discussions but would listen intently, usually not saying anything or getting involved, although we always invited her to join us.

One day while I was talking to a small group of women and telling them as long as there is breath in our bodies God has given us another chance, I saw Red sitting slightly behind me, listening intently. I turned so I could see her face, instead of having my back toward her. At that moment, for some reason which I don't fully comprehend, I felt this time and place was going to be Red's last chance at "getting right" something crucial in her life, between her and God. I got quiet for a moment, and for that moment there seemed to be just Red and me sitting there. Our eyes met and I quietly said to her, "Red, it is in my spirit to tell you that for you, this may well be your last chance to get it right between you and God. There is something you have let go far too long. I don't know what that is, but you do know." She kept her eyes fixed on mine for a long moment. Then she said, "Mrs. Smith, a couple of weeks before I got locked up my grandma, who is a strong Christian woman like you, had a long talk with me. Grandma said she felt I was going to have one last chance to get things right with God, and I know this is the time and place for me to do that." I was surprised that the words I had just spoken to her were a confirmation.

Sometime after that Red left. I have no way of knowing what happened to her, but I think of her sometimes, and I pray she did get it right between herself and the Lord, because one really never knows when we are on the last chance to get things right between us and God, since tomorrow or even the next moment is not promised to any of us.

As believers in Christ we know that God still speaks to us in many ways. He speaks to us through His written Word the Bible. He speaks through the still small voice inside of us, our spirits. He speaks through the Holy Spirit, and He speaks through other people, confirming what's already in our hearts. He still speaks, if we will listen. He is still the same God yesterday, today and forever, never changing (Hebrews 13:8).

My next cellmate had a wonderful sense of humor and nicknames for a few of the duty officers. There was one particular officer that she called jug head because he was sometimes disrespectful in his manner of speaking with the women. There was another officer that all the women were fond of, whom they called Doc. He was of retirement age, and a cancer survivor. He was well liked because he treated all the women fairly and with respect. When speaking to us he would say, "Ladies, I need your attention," instead of saying "Hey you," or "Inmates, quiet down," as jug head often did.

One afternoon, after lunch, both the upper and lower tiers were having quiet time resting in our cells, as we did each day. There were a few inmates who had been allowed in the day room, to do some cleaning and to help the duty officers. Doc was making rounds through the pod, checking each cell, and doing the afternoon inmate count. Other officers were at the desk, doing paperwork and chatting quietly amongst themselves. I had been reading on my top bunk and was just about to doze off for a nap when for some reason I abruptly sat up and focused on the stairs. There was nothing and no one on the stairs, but my eyes were fixed there. Thinking my cellmate was asleep I began to pray in the Spirit quietly, but audibly. My cellmate got up from her bunk and stood by the door of our cell, peering out. We watched as Doc began walking toward the stairs, looking down at his clipboard. As he began to descend the stairs he lost his balance, and began falling, head first, down the long, high metal stairs. He managed to grab the railing as he was falling, but not before seriously gashing his head. One of the officers at the desk hit the alarm as the inmates in the dayroom and other officers ran to help Doc. He remained conscious, although dazed, with blood flowing down his face. Officers and the inmates working in the day room grabbed clean white towels and began applying pressure to the wound. At least a dozen other officers swarmed into the pod, coming from every direction to help. Medical came rushing in with a stretcher, and Doc was swiftly taken out of the pod and to a local hospital. Many of us prayed for him. The duty officer allowed the women from both tiers to write get well wishes and prayers for Doc on a large poster board.

My cellmate and I made it a point to pray for Doc every day until we heard he was released from the hospital, and doing much better. One day, after he had gotten out of the hospital, he came to see all of us and thank us for what he said was the most beautiful card he'd ever received. Doc retired after that.

7

MORE OF THE UNEXPECTED

Every time I told myself nothing worst could possibly happen, something worst happened which would bring me to my knees and cause me to ask again, "Lord, why is all of this happening? Lord, don't you care that the bottom seems to have totally dropped out of my life and there appears to be no end in sight?"

Ms. O'Hara came to tell me the prosecutors were still offering Matt a plea deal if he would cooperate with them, and give names of the other accomplices. Matt said he would never be a snitch, even if it meant him taking the fall for others who were involved. I did not agree with him for taking such a stance, and felt he should cooperate. The allegations against him were grievous, without a doubt, and would ultimately cost him beyond anything any of us could have imagined.

By the time Matt's case went to trial in mid-July, the two accomplices had been identified by the police and arrested. They were Matt's friends Chris and Sean. Chris and Sean were also offered a plea deal if they would co-operate with the prosecutors. They accepted the plea deals they were offered and testified against Matt, saying everything had been his idea. They testified that a scuffle ensued between the eighteen-year old young man and Matt, and during the scuffle the young man was accidentally shot. They said they didn't realize he had been fatally wounded until several hours later, when they saw the police had cordoned off the area as a crime scene, and one of the neighbors told them a young man had been shot and killed. The murder was not premeditated, although the robbery had been planned. Chris and Sean's trials were held separately from Matt's. This information was devastating and it was extremely difficult for me to accept the fact that Matt had been involved in something that resulted in the death of another human being.

At the conclusion of Matt's trial he was convicted of first degree felony murder, in additional to numerous other charges. He would not be formally sentenced until the fall of the year. The two prosecutor's recommendation to the judge was for Matt to be given **two life sentences,** plus additional time. Two life sentences!! I was riveted by the thought, and I could not stop thinking about what that would mean for Matt.

Words could not begin to express the pain in my heart. I prayed I would be able to attend Matt's formal sentencing later in the fall of the year, since I had not been allowed to attend his trial.

I was told that the recommendation for Matt to be given two life sentences was because Matt tried to hire someone to kill a witness. I could not believe all I was hearing and reading in the newspaper. If these things were true of my son, he had totally gone in the opposite direction of how he was raised and what he knew in his heart was right.

As a mother I still felt that the recommended sentence was too much time for the actual crime. I asked myself, "Is it because Matt is African American that this sentence has been recommended? Is it because of the state that we live in? If this crime had happened in another state would the outcome have been the same?" No one will argue the fact that African American males are sentenced more often at a disproportionately higher rate than Caucasian males in our American legal system. I was vexed in my spirit and grieved beyond words.

Practically every woman in the pod was talking about Matt's case, even officers. My cellmate said, "Mrs. Smith, the women are saying even if Matt is guilty of all of those things, the sentence the prosecutors are recommending is an "over the top" sentence, and far too much time for the crime. You can count on the fact that Chris and Sean won't get anywhere near that type of sentence when their trials are held. They are not African American." Sadly, I had to agree with her because I knew her words were all too true. Sometime later Chris and Sean were each sentenced to approximately five years. Five years, versus two life sentences, when they all participated in the same crime?! Was this justice? Where was the fairness of their sentences versus what Matt was going to get?

Weeks earlier, before Matt's trial began, when I was still hoping against hope that it would somehow be proven that Matt was not involved in this situation to the extent the police said he was, I was sitting in the dayroom, flipping through the pages of an old Kenneth Copeland magazine, *The Believer's Voice of Victory*. Suddenly an article in the magazine drew my attention. It was called "Revival Is Rattling the Prison Walls," but what really drew my attention was a prophecy on the left side of the page, delivered by Kenneth Copeland at the Washington, D.C. Victory Campaign, ten years earlier, on February 3, 1994. The prophecy said:

> "I don't know who you are, or where you
> are…but there's somebody in this building, there's

> someone in your family who is going to the peni-
> tentiary. The Lord wanted me to tell you, 'Don't
> worry and wring your hands in concern, because I
> will watch over him, and I will be with him. I will
> deliver him and I will deliver him in better shape.
> I'll bring him back in better shape than when he
> left.' Don't cry over it anymore. I know it's hard to
> take, but don't cry over it anymore. This is not the
> end. This is the beginning."

Those words seemed to leap off the page and into my spirit, as I read and re-read them several times. I knew the Lord was speaking directly to me, preparing and reassuring me, weeks before Matt's trial that He was not going to abandon Matt or give up on him, even though he was going to the penitentiary.

Matt's attorney felt if the trial had been held in some other venue with a true jury of Matt's peers, as the law says, then the outcome would have been different. Although Matt's new attorney had requested a venue change, as well as additional time to prepare for the trial, the judge had denied both requests.

Friends and family who came into the jail to see Matt consistently told me he was depressed, remorseful and had "lost a considerable amount of weight." My pastor was greatly concerned about Matt's rapid and drastic loss of weight, and came to the jail often to talk with him and encourage him. Several other pastors whom our family had no affiliation with also visited him. Some of the male officers at the jail who were Christians would also talk to Matt. I would hear about it through the jail's news grapevine, as I liked to call it. I knew God was sending people to Matt, and I prayed Matt would listen to what the Lord was saying, not just with his ears, but with a contrite and repentant heart for what he had allowed himself to become involved in, and for all that had happened. I prayed he would remember no sin is too great for God to forgive.

I once heard a pastor say, "When we get to a place where we feel God is all we have, we begin to realize He is all we need." I wondered if Matt realized God was truly all he needed.

Matt asked Jesus into his heart and life at an early age, but somewhere during his teen years he allowed the things of the world to fill his heart and mind with its ideas of what he needed to do and be, in order to be successful. Matt had taken such a drastic detour from what he had been taught, and what he knew in his heart was the right thing to do. Satan tries to convince our young people that it's foolish to work hard and be honest, when you can sell drugs or your body and make money a lot faster; and like so many young people, Matt bought the lie and obviously did not count the cost of what would be required of him. Kay Arthur says in her book, *Lord, I Need Answers*, "Sin will take you further than you ever wanted to go, keep you longer than you ever wanted to stay, and cost you more than you ever expected to pay." So true!

In mid-August I got word that David's bond was revoked. He was rearrested and in addition to his charges of conspiracy and conspiracy to commit money laundering, he was being charged with perjury and all the charges that Matt had been convicted of. Since I was not permitted to attend Matt's trial while in jail, I was told that during the trial David refused to testify against Matt and repeatedly plead the Fifth Amendment. The prosecutors were livid with David and decided to charge him under the doctrine of "accessory to the crime." Their reasoning was that Matt, Chris and Sean had gone to David's home before and after committing their crime. I thought it just couldn't get worse than this; now with David facing murder charges. Oh, God!

About a week after David's bond was revoked Edward left the states permanently and relocated out of the country to join his new wife. I was so disappointed in him, not because he remarried, but because he had made little effort to be physically or emotionally available for any of his children during the past few months. He continued to send money each month, to Sarah, to put toward our bills. However, as far as giving of himself and his time, that was not happening. Julia and James went to see him the weekend before he left, although he told them he'd rather they didn't come because he was extremely busy. I was glad they went to see him. We had no way of knowing that it would be more than a decade before they would see him again.

On a Friday morning, several weeks after David's bond had been revoked, I was brought into court to be present for a motion Ms. O'Hara was presenting to once again try and get the judge to reconsider setting a bond for me. I had been in jail about three months. When I was brought into the courtroom, I was surprised to see James with his attorney. They were sitting at the table with Ms. O'Hara as I joined them. James had an expression on his face which indicated he was clearly troubled about something. Seated directly behind us were Chris' grandparents. I whispered to my attorney, "What is going on here?" Chris' grandparents sat with somber expressions on their faces, and avoided looking at me. We had known Chris' grandparents for years. Ms. O'Hara whispered to me that the prosecutors were now trying to also get James' bond revoked because Matt had sent a letter home and asked James to make sure Chris got the letter. Matt knew that Chris and Sean, like him, were still in jail. However, since inmates are not allowed to write to each other directly, they will usually send a letter to someone, outside of the jail, and have that person re-mail the letter back into the jail to the designated person. James, not knowing the contents of Matt's letter to Chris, hand delivered it to Chris' grandparents' home and asked Chris' grandpa to mail it back to the jail to Chris. Chris' grandpa decided to open the letter, knowing it was from Matt. When Chris' grandpa read the letter he took it to the office of the prosecutors. In the letter Matt threatened Chris. What in the world was Matt thinking?! It was clear James had not opened the letter, and therefore he had no way of knowing the contents of the letter, but the prosecutors did not care about that. They simply wanted James' bond revoked for delivering the letter. This could not be happening!

Thankfully James' bond was not revoked that day because the judge wanted time to think about the prosecutors' request. In the meantime, Ms. O'Hara was allowed to present her motion, once again, asking the court to allow me to be bonded out. The discussion of my case ran over, in time, and the court adjourned until Monday, when we were all scheduled to be back in court.

Over the weekend I talked to James and told him just in case his bond happened to get revoked on Monday that he should take care of some things in the next couple of days with regards to his job, Julia, and our house. He said his attorney did not foresee his bond being revoked. I told him to prepare for the unexpected. I also talked with Julia and Lauren. For the past couple of weeks Julia had been staying at our house everyday instead of at Sarah's since I had allowed Lauren to stay there during Matt's trial. I told the girls that in the event James' bond was revoked on Monday, Julia would not be allowed to stay at the house with just Lauren, but would have to go to the Latimer's home full time, and I told Lauren she would have to leave and make other arrangements. Julia was not happy and protested saying she was fine with Lauren, who had recently turned eighteen, and I needed to learn to trust her. I explained to Julia that this was not about trusting her, but about her safety and wellbeing, and my peace of mind in knowing she would be with an adult whom I trusted. The Latimers were wonderful, close, Christian friends whom I had known for over a decade. They were open to taking Julia and giving Sarah a break.

On Monday I was brought back to court to continue what had been discussed on Friday. I was waiting in the holding area and expecting at any moment the bailiff would come in and call my name. The door of courtroom swung open but instead of the bailiff calling my name, James was being escorted to a holding cell. His face was pale, as he removed his belt from his trousers, and handed it to the bailiff. It had already been decided for him! His bond had been revoked! I felt awful for James. I began to cry uncontrollably and call on the Name of the Lord. "Jesus, Jesus, Jesus. Oh God, have mercy. What in the world is going on?" I keenly felt the hurt and pain I saw in James' face.

Shortly, I was called into the courtroom. I listened through teary eyes as the judge once again denied bond for me, saying, "Mrs. Smith, I remand you to the court. You will return to the jail. You are dismissed." Every effort that Ms. O'Hara made to get me bonded out had proven to be futile, and once again there were four family members in jail.

Sarah had been a tremendous help with Julia but needed a break. However, she would continue to be my Power of Attorney. Other friends offered to take Julia, but I knew Julia would be happy with the Latimers because they had a daughter a year older than Julia.

After James' bond was revoked, I called the Latimers, Sarah, and Debbie as soon as I got back to the pod from court. I called my house and spoke to Julia and Lauren. I told Lauren she would have to leave immediately and I told Julia that Sarah would be over shortly, to take her to the Latimer's home. Sarah was instructed that our house should be locked up and utilities turned off indefinitely. I knew Sarah and Debbie never trusted Lauren being there with Julia, and they both suspected Lauren might be in the same line of work Matt had been involved in. Lauren said she was fine with whatever I wanted her to do, and said she could quickly make other arrangements. I was glad for her that she had other options. I had no way of knowing what Lauren was involved in. I was thankful for the Latimers stepping in to take responsibility for Julia's wellbeing. Their kindness meant so much to me.

8

TROUBLE IN THE CELL

After David and James' bonds were revoked, within just a few weeks of each other, I was more depressed than I had been the entire time I was at the jail. I tried to wrap my mind around the fact that sadly, all four of us were once again in jail, in addition to Chris and Sean. I also heard other arrests had been made for people whom I did not know, but who were in some way connected to Matt's case. I continued to try to go about my usual routine of getting up early each morning to pray. The cellmate I currently had was the only cellmate who complained about me getting up early and praying. I didn't care if she complained because I knew I wasn't disturbing her. Therefore, I wasn't about to change my habit of early morning prayer to accommodate her. Though she didn't like what I did, the two of us had managed to get along. That was about to change.

Since our pod was the only section in the entire jail to house female inmates, there were times on the weekends when every cell was filled, as well as the cells in the holding area, and still there would be women coming in, charged with things like drunk and disorderly conduct or driving while intoxicated. When all the cells filled, the officers would begin putting three women to a cell. When a third woman was brought into an already small cell, needless to say, there was barely room to walk in the cell. Something called a "boat" would be brought into the cell, which resembled a blue canoe with a thin foam mattress for the third person to sleep on. There had never been a third woman in any of the cells I had been in.

That changed and our cell was selected two weekends in a row, by the duty officer, as the overflow cell for a third female. We were told to make room. The second time we were selected wasn't for a new inmate, but for Big Liz from the bottom tier. Liz was open about the fact that she was a lesbian, and I had no issue with what she did in her personal life, but what I did have an issue with was the filth that came out of her mouth. This time I was not happy. Never had I complained about any cellmate, nor had I ever complained when being moved from top tier to bottom and back again. I prayed, "Lord, give me a Christ-like attitude toward Liz. Help me to be able to witness to her." My cellmate, Shelley, on the other hand was delighted that Liz was coming to our cell. Liz was being moved because her mate had been arrested, was in the holding area, and about to be brought into the main population. The duty officer did not want Liz and her mate on the same tier. Liz was irate that her mate had been arrested for what she termed "some ridiculous petty charges" and equally unhappy about having to move from the lower tier, to the upper, and be on a boat, as a third person in the cell. I was unhappy too, about the prospect of having her in our cell because I had heard the filth that came out of her mouth. Nonetheless, as she came up the stairs cussing, fussing, stumping, complaining and dragging her blue tote behind her, Shelley and I stepped outside of the cell and gave her a hand with her things. She came into the cell and immediately said to me, "Mrs. Smith, I respect you a lot. I'm sure you know I am a lesbian, and I have a terrible mouth. I don't mean no harm to nobody. This is just me, and right now I'm mad as hell, but I'm gonna try to watch my mouth. So, I'm just gonna apologize to you in advance for what you're gonna be hearing me say." I nodded my head, and said, "Liz, I appreciate you being candid with me, and I'm going to be honest with you. I wish you didn't have to be in the cell with us, just as much as you wish you could have stayed downstairs. I am a born again Christian, as you know. I don't cuss and I don't appreciate when someone spouts off obscenity and filth in my presence. I understand you're upset right now, but I would very much appreciate it if you would do your best to try and refrain from cussing around me." We both had our say. Liz tried for a few minutes but the cussing was so much a part of her vocabulary that she couldn't seem to complete a sentence without using a cuss word. I cringed each time I heard what came out of her mouth. Even when she tried to clean it up, it was still bad. She and Shelley got along fabulously. Shelley laughed heartily each time Liz cussed, and even joined Liz with the cussing. I tried to ignore them by reading.

In order for Liz to be moved out of our cell, somebody would have to go home, and no one was scheduled to go home anytime soon. The pod was overly full. In order for me to move out of the cell with Liz and Shelley, I would need to submit paperwork to the duty officer, who would then submit it to her supervisor. The process usually took anywhere from ten days to two weeks, and one could still be denied the request to move. I knew for a fact that several females on our tier had put in written requests, weeks earlier, asking to either be given a different cellmate or to be moved to the other tier and most of them were still waiting, and barely avoiding a physical confrontation with their cellmates.

It had become my practice, at the jail, at bedtime to take my sheet and blanket and completely cover my face and head in order to go to sleep. When I was home I never did that, but here I felt it allowed me to shut out everyone and everything around me, if only for a few brief hours; and the other reason I covered my head was it was usually freezing in the pod at night so by putting my head under the cover I stayed much warmer during the night.

Psalm 4:8 says, "I will lie down and sleep in peace, for you alone, O Lord, make me dwell in safety." I usually slept quite soundly at night at the jail, and had occasionally slept right through fights in nearby cells. The women laughed at me, and said, "Mrs. Smith can sleep through just about anything in here. It has to be incredibly loud to disturb her."

On our first night of having Liz as our new cellmate as I prepared to go to sleep, Shelley and Liz were having a grand time, laughing, talking loudly, cussing, telling filthy jokes, and hollering at the top of their voices out of the cell door to Liz's mate on the lower tier. I tried to shut out their noise, but tossed and turned for hours before finally drifting off to sleep, only to be jolted awake periodically by their loud, hyena laughter, and cussing. They were inconsiderate of everyone around them. During the night I vaguely heard others banging on the walls telling Shelley and Liz, not so nicely, to be quiet, so others could sleep. Shelley and Liz ignored any and all requests to be quiet. I tossed and turned most of the night.

The next morning I sleepily got up at my usual time to pray quietly. I went through my morning routine of washing up, getting dressed, and then praying quietly. As I was pacing back and forth by the toilet and the door, praying softly, Shelley sat up on her bunk and said, "Why in the world are you up so early praying?

Don't you see we are trying to sleep? This is ridiculous! You get up every morning and do this. Oh, my goodness! This is so inconsiderate!" I could not believe she was saying this to me. For a few minutes I forgot to be Christ-like in my response and had to restrain myself from grabbing her and slapping her. My words exploded on her like Fourth of July fireworks. "You have the audacity to call me inconsiderate, Shelley?! Have you lost your mind? Did I say anything to you and Liz last night when the two of you were hollering through the cell door at the top of your lungs cussing, laughing and talking like it was two in the afternoon instead of two in the morning? Did I, Shelley? Did I, Liz?" Liz had by then sat up on her boat, rubbing sleep out of her eyes and yawning. "You're not bothering me by praying, Mrs. Smith. I'm not in this. This is between you and Shelley." Shelley and I began a loud and heated exchange of words, each calling the other inconsiderate. The women in the adjoining cells began banging on the walls and asking, "Mrs. Smith, are you okay, over there? What is going on?" The duty officer came to our cell and said, "Ladies, ladies, what is going on in there?" Shelley and I were both trying to talk to him at the same time. He shrugged his shoulders, yawned, and walked back to his desk, telling us to take the volume down on our argument, since most of the women were still trying to sleep. He mumbled something about his shift being almost over, so let the morning shift officer handle it. Shelley and I glared at each other a few minutes but didn't have anything further to say. I continued pacing the floor, close to tears, but still praying. I had to repent for getting so angry with her that I could have easily gotten into a physical altercation with her.

When we came out of our cells for breakfast, the women said, "Mrs. Smith, we've never heard you raise your voice before. My goodness, you've certainly got spunk." They chuckled. I did not laugh because I was angry with Shelley and Liz, and quite frankly, embarrassed that I had lost my temper with Shelley.

During breakfast many of the women told Liz and Shelley they were extremely rude and inconsiderate the night before, and should be ashamed of themselves. Liz and Shelley didn't try to defend themselves, nor did they apologize. The two of them put their heads down and quietly ate breakfast. I was quiet during breakfast as well. Maybe I should have handled it differently, in a more Christ-like manner, I thought.

After breakfast, when Liz, Shelley and I returned to the cell Shelley climbed back into her bunk and Liz back onto her boat. The two of them lay quietly with their eyes closed. I knew they were not asleep. The pod was freezing that morning so I wrapped myself in my extra blanket and continued to pace the floor, praying softly.

A few minutes later an unexpected thing happened. One of the officers who drove the transport van came into our pod. He told me on several occasions when he saw me going to court that he and some of the other officers were praying for my family, and that some of the officers had spoken to Matt about the mess he was involved in, and asked him how in the world had he allowed his family to be dragged into something we were not a part of.

As the transport officer came down the hall some of the women began calling out his name, howling, flirting and talking to him through their cell doors. Liz jumped up from her boat and went the cell door. He was one of her favorites, too. As he came closer to our cell she called out to him. He responded back to her with, "Well hello, Miss Liz; and how are you doing? Are you behaving yourself?" She put on her best act and nodded her head innocently. He looked again and saw me standing slightly behind her. "Hey, Mrs. Smith. How are you doing?" Suddenly I began to cry. I could not manage to get any words out of my mouth, but tears streamed down my face. He hollered to the duty officer to pop open the cell right away. As they popped the cell door he pulled me out into the hallway. "What in the world is wrong, Mrs. Smith?" Through sobs I began to tell him about Shelley and Liz the night before, all the cussing, laughing, hollering, and filthy jokes. Women from other cells gathered and began telling him it was terrible the night before with Liz and Shelley. He glared at Liz and Shelley. "Mrs. Smith, do you want to be moved out of there?" I nodded my head yes, as he called for one of the other officers. Officer Davis came up the steps saying there were other women who had issues with their cellmates who were waiting to be moved, and the pod was overly crowded. The transport officer told Officer Davis, "Mrs. Smith is going through some incredibly serious stuff right now, as I'm sure you, and every officer in this pod, are well aware of. The last thing she needs right now, on top of what she has to deal with, is two people like this in a cell with her. Let's get her out of there, right now!" Officer Davis told the transport officer he needed to speak to Officer Blake, who was in charge that morning. She was called and the transport officer told her what happened the night before with Liz and Shelley. Without a moments hesitation she said, "Get your things, Smith. I'm going to move you. Let me juggle some people, and I will get you in with a good cellmate. You will stay on this tier, and go over on the other side of the hallway with Susan." I thanked her and the transport officer profusely, but I especially thanked God for His quick and divine intervention.

In less than fifteen minutes I had a new cellmate. Susan got my tote and carried it to the cell I would share with her. I knew the Lord had sent the transport officer that morning to our pod. In the months I had been at the jail the transport officer had never come to our pod. Today I was immensely thankful, and I knew it

was again the hand, the favor, the mercy, and the divine intervention of God.

For the next couple of days Shelley and Liz ignored me, and I
ignored them, but the Holy Spirit convicted me, and said I could
not be an effective witness for Christ, if I continued to be angry
with them for their immaturity and inconsideration. So I went to
both of them and said, "Ladies, let's not have any hard feelings between us. Maybe we all could have handed the situation somewhat
differently. I apologize." I believe they were relieved, and agreed,
"No hard feelings, Mrs. Smith. We apologize also." I was happy
we were able to forgive each other.

After that Shelley, who doesn't like to walk, decided she wanted to walk with me in the pod, at least once a day. I felt I was able
to witness for Christ much more effectively with her after that, and
I truly didn't have any hard feelings toward either of them.

About a week later, Shelley and Liz got into a big argument
because Liz became so loud and obnoxious that even Shelley got
tired of it and asked to be moved to another cell. Officer Blake
ignored Shelley's request and left them together. Sometime later
Liz was moved out of the pod to participate in a program for ha-
bitual drug offenders. She would be housed in a different part of
the building and would not come back, unless she messed up. We
knew she was not trying to mess up in the new program because
doing well meant she stood a good chance of getting her sentence
reduced when she went to court again.

My cellmate, Susan, was a young woman in her early twenties.
She had a beautiful singing voice. She and I would talk about the
Lord and sing Christian songs in the cell. Some days, even with all
the praying and fasting that I did I would allow myself to get into
a low, self-pitying mood. Susan would notice, and would start to
sing. One of the songs she sang, which I especially liked, was by

Fred Hammond. Some of the lyrics were, "There should be a fire in your heart when you praise, consuming every part because you know the God you serve will make His presence known, when you praise Him." That song reminded me there is power not only in our prayers, but more importantly, in our praises. I started adding praises to my prayers, even when I did not feel like praising. Sometimes I would just say, "Lord, I praise You for who You are. I praise you that nothing, absolutely nothing, is too difficult or impossible for You. It does not matter how bleak the circumstances appear to be. I will praise You and trust You always." God's Word says in Psalms 22:3 that He inhabits the praises of His people. We must learn to send our praises up to God even before we send our petitions and requests, because praise breaks through the wall of that impossible situation we are facing when nothing else can. It is no sacrifice to praise God on a Sunday morning, in church, surrounded by other believers, when all is going well in our lives.

Kenneth Copeland said, "There has never been a problem that intimidates God, and Satan has never devised a problem that faith in God cannot fix." How comforting that is to know.

In Revelation 2:13 God says, "I know where you live…" and certainly He knew exactly where I was living physically, emotionally and spiritually at that moment. He knew!

Susan went home and Fanny became my cellmate. Fanny was to be my last cellmate, although I had no way of knowing it.

9

ANOTHER ARREST AND LICE IN THE POD

On September 14th, about two weeks after James' bond was revoked, I got another unexpected jolt. That afternoon while I was sitting in the day room reading, a young woman named Charlotte came rushing over to me. "Mrs. Smith, Mrs. Smith Lauren has been arrested. I just talked to her and she asked me to tell you she is here." I stared at Charlotte. I could not manage to get any words out of my mouth. Charlotte grabbed me by the hand and said, "Come on, Mrs. Smith, I will show you." She practically pulled me toward the holding area and sure enough, there stood Lauren. I don't know who cried first, me or Lauren, but we both burst in tears. She looked terrible, with deep, dark circles under her eyes and she was very thin. "Lauren, why in the world are you here? What has happened to you?" I asked her.

Through tears Lauren began trying to explain what happened. She said she had been arrested in a hotel room, with two other people, and charged with "possession of cocaine, with the intent to distribute." She had gone to the hotel room to give her friend money to help with her baby and had only been there a few minutes when the police burst into the room. There was cocaine in a drawer in the room, she explained, saying she had no way of knowing it was there. To me, it was a believable story. I felt badly for Lauren, but I was immensely relieved that Julia had not been with her, and thankful that I had made the decision several weeks earlier to have Sarah lock up my house and have Julia stay with the Latimers.

That evening when my cellmate Fanny and I were talking, Fanny said she wasn't buying Lauren's story for one second. Fanny said if she were a betting person she would wager it was Lauren's "product" in the hotel room drawer, and her guess was Lauren had been selling as well as using. I wanted to believe Lauren but I knew Fanny was street-wise and not as naïve as I was. Fanny said she could write a book about dealing and using drugs, because she had at one time been involved in that lifestyle.

Still, I struggled with believing Lauren was using or selling drugs. Lauren had been given a second chance to get out and stay out of the legal entanglement. She sat through Matt's entire trial and heard everything, including the recommendation for him to be given two life sentences. Hadn't any of that made an impact on her? Sarah and Debbie had long suspected Lauren was not an innocent bystander but had her hands just as deeply in the dirt of the drug business as Matt, Chris and Sean. For the first time I began to think that maybe, just maybe, Sarah, Debbie, and Fanny were right about Lauren. I was definitely getting an education in some things while I was incarcerated, and slowly, but surely, learning not to be naive. If I still had any doubts about the extent of Lauren's involvement in the drug business, I had only to wait, and later events would prove beyond any doubt that Debbie, Sarah and Fanny had always been right.

Fanny was a wonderful, considerate cellmate with a great sense of humor. Sometimes she even managed to make me laugh when all I wanted to do was to curl up in a corner and nurse my wounds and pain. Someone else had led Fanny to accept Jesus as Lord and Savior shortly before she came to jail. However, since she was new in having a relationship with Jesus Christ she was full of questions about how to get closer to the Living God. Fanny said she used to have "religion" because as a child her mom made her and her siblings go to church, just to get them out of the house. She said once she considered God to be a "God for Sunday, and for when you really got into trouble." Now, however, she understood she could have a personal relationship with the Lord, and that He is a God who desires to be intimately acquainted with us every moment of our lives. Fanny and I talked about the Lord, and the fact that Christians aren't perfect, just forgiven. We read and discussed the Bible every day.

Fanny was also a tray server like several of my previous cellmates had been. Fanny, too, made a point of making sure I had something "good" to eat at least once a day, which was usually some fresh fruit or a couple of slices of whole wheat bread. Fanny was scheduled to go home sometime in early October. She encouraged me that I was going home, too. "Now, Mrs. Smith, *when* you get out of this place, you've gotta come see me and meet my mother. She will love you." I promised her I would do that. She was from a large family, but of all of her siblings she felt she was closest with her mother, who was terminally ill. Her siblings told her their mom was weak and barely holding onto life, but asked about her every day. Fanny's prayer was that God would not allow her mom to die before she got home. We prayed every night for God to sustain Fanny's mom, at least until Fanny came home.

One Sunday when Fanny and I and the majority of the women in the pod had gone to the afternoon church service, the minister led us in a song called, "Coming Up on the Rough Side of the Mountain." Later, after church, I told Fanny some of us weren't just coming up on the rough side of the mountain, but had been on the rough side of the mountain far too long, and were anxious to get to the other side. We laughed heartily in agreement.

We often think of peace as the absence of trouble or confusion in our lives, or a time when the circumstances of our lives are in harmony with the people and things around us, but it is so much more. The Bible speaks much about peace. In fact, there are over two hundred scriptures that speak about peace. One of my favorite passages is a simple, yet profound, word found in Philippians 4:7. It says, "And the peace of God, which transcends all understanding, will guard you hearts and your minds." I have learned that is the kind of peace which can only come from having an intimate relationship with our heavenly Father. There were days when I had that kind of peace "which transcends all understanding" and there were days when I let that kind of peace slip away, feeling as if we (my family) were in the boat alone, in the very eye of the storm with no rescue in sight. I knew Satan wanted me to feel alone, abandoned, and hopeless, but I reminded myself that with God, all things are possible, and we were not abandoned or hopeless.

How do we get that kind of peace and keep it? Isaiah 26:3 says (paraphrased), "God will keep in perfect peace the one whose mind is stayed upon the Him because our trust is in Him." We obtain that kind of peace by staying in God's Word, praying and meditating on the Word, and not the circumstances or the problem. That is the challenge for each of us, and it was a huge challenge for me.

I once heard a minister say, "There have been some battles that I have engaged in on my own and have pitifully lost, but there have been many battles that the Lord has fought on my behalf, and had He not fought those battles for me, I would have been totally wiped out because Satan had his best shots aimed at me." That is how I felt. I knew beyond a doubt that unless the Lord fought this battle for me and my family, we were without hope.

One night, as the women were in the day room talking, watching TV and doing each other's hair, a new inmate who had been there about a week sat, awaiting her turn for someone to braid her hair. She was a young, attractive college student from the local university, with long blond hair, that she wore twirled in a bun. The woman who was going to braid for her began combing through the hair, and within seconds blurted out, "Oh my goodness, honey! You've got lice!! Everyone sitting within a ten-foot radius immediately moved away from her, and someone rushed off to the duty officer's desk to tell her. The officer called medical and in just a few minutes a nurse came into the pod. She examined "Blondie's" hair, using gloves, and then confirmed the obvious. The news went through the pod like a wild fire and the result was near chaos. Several women gathered around her, asking her why she hadn't used the de-louse shampoo when she came through intake. She began to cry, saying she had used the de-louse shampoo. They told her she was lying. Some of the women began cussing at her and saying unkind things. The young woman was removed from the pod and taken to medical. Several hours later she returned to the pod with freshly washed hair and a new, short haircut, along with a product she was told to use daily for a week.

In the meantime, the decision was made by the nurse and the duty officer that every woman in every cell, upper and lower tiers, and everything in every cell, would have to be thoroughly cleaned and deloused, regardless of whether we had any contact with Blondie or not. It was 9:30 p.m., and some of us were almost ready to go to bed. We were told to strip all beds and get everything ready to be sent to laundry. Everything that could be washed would be. It became a huge production. Other officers were brought into the pod to help coordinate the massive undertaking. The jail's laundry room, which was normally closed in the evening, was opened up for the women's pod, and the voluminous amounts of laundry. Enormous laundry containers were brought into the pod as everyone sorted, labeled, and loaded laundry into the containers.

In the meantime, we were called cell by cell to the showers and given delouse liquid to shampoo our hair, as well as to use on our bodies. As we came out of the showers we were issued a clean uniform, and a pair of white cotton panties, but no bra. Many of the women were blatantly angry about the inconvenience to everyone, and the fact that this young woman, who had been in the pod about a week, had managed to get through the intake process at the jail with no one detecting the fact that she had a serious case of head lice. Prior to this evening she had not been seen by medical. It would be fair to say the jail's policy changed that night. Thereafter women processing into the jail were sent directly from intake to medical, which is how it should have always been.

There were many angry words and more than a few cuss words directed toward Blondie. She was in tears when she left the pod and when she returned. She did not get a lot of sympathy from any of the women, the officers, or even her cellmate, who requested to be immediately moved out of the cell they shared. Each cell had to be thoroughly cleaned, which required us getting down on hands and knees using disinfectant to clean floors, toilets, and wiping down the bunk beds. By about 3:30 a.m., I was totally exhausted and could barely keep my eyes open. Our cell was finished, and so were all the cells on our tier. Our tier was inspected and passed. However, there was still a tremendous amount of activity in the pod with people going back and forth passing out the clean laundry that had just begun arriving back in the pod. Our cell's linens had not arrived back from the laundry, but I was too tired to care. I lay exhausted on the cold, thin, blue vinyl mattress, without a sheet, blanket, or pillow. Almost immediately I began to doze off. Vaguely I heard my cellmate saying, "Mrs. Smith, your blanket is here. I'm going to put it over you, alright?" I managed to mumble an extremely tired 'thank you' as I was covered with the clean, warm blanket.

The next morning when the pod officer sleepily called breakfast only a few of us managed to get up. Blondie was teary eyed and apologetic for several days, but the lice episode was not soon forgotten, and no one volunteered to do her hair after that.

10

THE PLEA OFFER, THE RELEASE

One morning in mid-September while having prayer and reading the Bible these words repeatedly welded up in my spirit: "Suddenly, in a little while, and with great joy." I asked the Holy Spirit, "What will be suddenly, in a little while, and with great joy??" Almost as quickly as I asked the question, I knew the answer in my spirit. The answer was soon, unexpectedly, and with great joy, I would go home. "Suddenly, in a little while, and with great joy." I repeated those words several times. I knew God's timing is not necessarily my timing, and suddenly to Him might be a little different than I would want suddenly to be. I personally wanted suddenly to be in the next ten minutes that I'd be walking out of the doors of the jail. Nonetheless, with joy I received and thanked the Lord for the words of encouragement that I would go from this place, "suddenly, in a little while, and with great joy."

I shared those words with my friends, Dorothy and Carolyn, who came to see me that same day during visitation. Dorothy said our pastor's sermon topic for the past couple of Sundays had been the word "suddenly." She said he talked about how things happen in life suddenly, unexpectedly, and how we are most often unprepared. I agreed. David, James and I had certainly been arrested suddenly, on that Friday, May 28th. Matt had been found suddenly, in New Jersey, and extradited back to our state. I could think of a dozen other things that had happened suddenly in our lives in the last couple of weeks and months. Dorothy, Carolyn and I agreed that rarely are any of us prepared for those "suddenly" moments.

About a week later, on Friday, September 24th, I received a message from the duty officer to call my attorney's office right away. I called and immediately got Allison, Ms. O'Hara's secretary. There was an excitement in Allison's voice that I hadn't heard in the four months I had been at the jail. She was usually quiet and reserved, and even apologetic that they hadn't been able to get the judge to release me. On that Friday, however, the words tumbled excitedly out of her mouth. "Diana, the Commonwealth is drawing up a plea offer for you to consider. Today! Now! Even as we speak! Ms. O'Hara wanted me to let you know she will come into the jail on Monday, September, 27th, around 10:00 a.m., to see you and explain the plea offer to you. Diana, this is just wonderful! We have wanted them to make an offer to us, for you, but as you are well aware of, they have not until now."

I had Allison repeat everything, to be sure I heard her correctly. I thanked her, hung up the phone, prayed silently, and walked through the pod in kind of daze for a few minutes, as I repeated Allison's words to myself. The prosecutor is even now drawing up a plea offer which Ms. O'Hara will explain to me on Monday at 10:00 a.m. This is what Ms. O'Hara's office has wanted for me.

Some part of me said, "Don't get your hopes up too high. You've been disappointed before when your attorney's office has tried unsuccessfully to get you out." This time, though, there was an excitement rising up from someplace deep within me, like a giant wave coming up from the bottom of the ocean floor, and what I heard in my spirit was, "Now, see God move on your behalf. Go ahead and get your hopes up high. Go ahead, and dare to believe the Awesome God you serve, Who still specializes in things thought impossible, and Who will surely make His Presence known." Psalm 25:5 says, "and my hope is in you all day long." I wanted to shout out loud, "Yes, thank you Lord. My hope and trust are in you all day long." Instead I did my best to remain low key, with just a slight smile on my face, as I continued to think about the conversation I'd just had with Allison. I decided to take a slow walk through the pod. A couple of the women asked, "Are you alright Mrs. Smith?" "Yes, yes, I'm fine," I said. "I think I'll just go back to my cell. I'll talk to you ladies later on."

I asked the guard to please open my cell, and I went back in so I could really talk to the Lord. My cellmate, Fanny was still in class. I began to pace back and forth in the cell and praise and thank the Lord, and rejoice out loud. "Hallelujah, Lord, Hallelujah. It is done, in Your Name. It is done. Amen!" As I praised Him, I could just hear Satan saying, "Now aren't you being a bit premature here? Why are you getting your hopes up? You don't even know *what kind* of plea offer is going to be made to you. What if…." I ignored the "what if" and just kept right on praising and thanking God for the wonderful miracle I felt was about to unfold. I praised and thanked Him as if it was already done!

I considered telling my cellmate about the plea offer being prepared for me when she came back from her Anger Management class, but I changed my mind because I didn't want to hear anything negative from anyone. I wanted to keep my faith high and my eyes on the Lord, and see His hand move, on my behalf. I decided I would not tell anyone and I would try to take my mind off the conversation with Allison by cleaning out my blue tote. I hummed a tune and told myself I was cleaning out the tote in preparation for Monday's inspection. As I cleaned the tote, I made a mental note of what would go out of the jail with me, should I be released, and what I would leave for the women. It was sort of an unwritten courtesy among the women, when anyone was leaving to go home, they would leave some of their things to the women who remained, who had the greatest needs among us. There were some women who didn't have money on canteen to purchase things they needed, because they didn't have anyone sending money to them. Many women had blessed me in the four months I had been there and I knew I wanted to be a blessing to some of them when I left. I decided Lauren would get my long johns since she complained she was freezing every night. I knew Fanny would want my hair and hygiene products, and there were other things in my tote that I would give to some of the other women.

I finished cleaning my tote as Fanny returned from class. I felt I would burst if I didn't tell her of my conversation with Allison. However, I surprised myself and didn't say anything even remotely connected to my earlier conversation with Allison. Instead we talked about how Fanny's Anger Management class had been and about the excitement she felt, knowing she was going home in a couple of weeks. Fanny said she was looking forward to spending time with her mom, her children and grandchildren, but especially her new boyfriend.

Later that evening I called Debbie collect. We talked, and she told me that Sharon, who leads the intercessor prayer team at our church, had asked church members, who were willing, to please pray and fast for me on that Friday evening. I asked Debbie to thank Sharon and all the others who were willing to fast and continue to pray for me. I had fasted so much during the four months of being incarcerated. Fasting, honestly, has never been one of my favorite things to do, so I did it out of absolute necessity. I didn't even tell Debbie about my conversation with Allison. I continued to pray in the spirit asking the Lord to help me walk by faith that something wonderful was about to happen. I told the Lord I would be at peace no matter what the outcome would be. I tried to focus on other things so I wouldn't keep thinking about Allison's conversation, and the fact that Monday was three whole days away. I prayed again, "Lord, I have put the outcome of this plea offer into the most capable hands I know. Yours, Lord. I ask that Your perfect will prevail for me, and my children, and I thank you in advance for Your mercy and kindness toward us."

The weekend seemed to go by exceedingly slow. On Sunday I went to church. I talked to and prayed with some of the women, wrote a few letters, read an entire book, and started a new one. I made it through another weekend with God's help, just as I had done for the past four months.

Monday, September 27th finally came. We began our usual daily routine of breakfast, cleaning our cells, and then our weekly Monday morning cell and tote inspection. Afterward Fanny went to her Anger Management class. While she was gone, I paced back and forth in the cell, praying in the Spirit, interceding, and talking to the Lord. Periodically I looked at the big wall clock in the pod. Ten o'clock came and went and Ms. O'Hara had not shown up. Allison said I could expect Ms. O'Hara at around ten o'clock. I tried not to be concerned, and I tried not to look at the clock every few minutes, but it was now almost 11:00 o'clock. I walked back and forth in the cell and continued to pray, intercede and talk to the Lord. I rebuked every doubt that Satan tried to put in my mind.

Suddenly, right before lunch time, the duty officer buzzed my cell through the intercom and said, "Smith, get ready for the transport to court." I thought there must have been some mistake. I wasn't scheduled for court. So I pressed the intercom and told her I was not scheduled for court. She repeated, "Smith, they want you in court NOW, so get ready for court NOW!" I got ready. As I got ready, I replayed in my head the conversation I'd had with Allison on Friday. She hadn't said anything about court. She said Ms. O'Hara would be in to see me, around 10:00 a.m., to explain the terms of the plea agreement. I finished tying up my sneakers, and went into the day room to tell the duty officer I was ready to be transported. I was the only person on the transport being taken to court.

The officer transporting me was none other than the wonderful officer whom God had used to get me moved out of the cell with Shelley and Big Liz several weeks earlier. He talked as we drove along and told me he had seen my three sons recently, and they were well. He said, "Mrs. Smith, it's a shame you've had to be here four months, and you weren't allowed to be bonded out. I just don't understand that. I truly hope your son, Matt, realizes what he has put you and your family through, and your great sacrifice for him." I didn't respond with words to his comments. I couldn't. I looked down at my hands, and held back the tears.

We arrived at the court and followed the usual procedure. The transport officer turned me over to the bailiff as I was put in a holding cell and waited to be called. I wondered where Ms. O'Hara was. I kept thinking she was supposed to come see me at 10:00 a.m., at the jail. Were the prosecuting attorneys having me brought to court without my attorney being present? Suddenly the door leading from the courtroom to the holding area swung open, and Ms. O'Hara came rushing through with a big smile on her face. "Diana, the prosecuting attorneys have prepared an offer for us. I apologize that I didn't get to come over to the jail this morning to explain it to you first, but I wanted to expedite things and get you over here, now." She began reading the plea offer to me. "If you accept the plea offer you will be released with time served. There will be a condition of good behavior for a period of one year, court fines, and a felony." I heard the word felony and began to panic. "A felony!? But I don't want a felony on my record at fifty-four years old, Ms. O'Hara. I have had an excellent record my entire life, with a top secret security clearance when I was in the military." She stared at me for a moment, and quietly said, "This is the offer they are making to us, Diana. It is entirely your choice." "What do you think, Ms. O'Hara? Do you think it's a good offer?" "I think it's a good offer, yes. I don't think the felony is going to make much of a difference for you, Diana, in terms of you getting work because you always present yourself well." "But what about my sons, Mrs. O'Hara? Will David and James be made the same offer?" "Yes, they will, later in the week. The prosecutors wanted to offer it to you first." I thought for a moment longer, and then I asked her one final question. "Will I go home today, Ms. O'Hara?" Excitedly she replied, "Yes, today, Diana. Today!" In that same moment I heard the still small voice of the Lord speaking His reassurance within me. I heard Him say, "Don't be afraid or concerned about a felony. What is a felony to Me but ink on paper! For I will still open doors for you that no man can open, and I will close where I do not desire you to be." With that reassurance from my Father I was at peace. "Ms. O'Hara, tell them I'll take it." She smiled, winked her eye, nodded her head, and dashed out of the door, back toward the courtroom.

In less than a minute I was ushered quickly into the courtroom by the bailiff,   and seated at a large table next to my attorney, facing a judge whom I did not recognize. Ms. O'Hara reiterated again what was about to happen, and what I would be asked. She said I was under no pressure whatsoever from anyone to accept the plea offer. It was strictly up to me.

I had expected to see Judge Mayfield who had been the judge for Matt, David, James and me throughout this ordeal. To my complete surprise there was a different judge presiding, from a neighboring county. I was asked to please stand and state my full name. My attorney and I arose, simultaneously, and stood shoulder to shoulder. This judge was extremely kind to me, and not in the least bit abrupt or condescending in the way Judge Mayfield had been. This judge made sure I understood everything, in lay terms. He made sure I had not been in any way pressured or coerced to sign the plea offer. I was polite, as I always tried to be, and said 'yes sir, no sir,' in response to all of his questions. Then I heard the judge say, "Mrs. Smith, you are released from the custody of the county jail. You are free! However, you will need to return to the jail for a few minutes to go through the out processing procedure, and to retrieve your personal belongings that are still in possession of the jail. I wish you the best of luck, Mrs. Smith. I see that you have no previous record of any kind. I am not sure why you were held for four months on these charges. It is unfortunate that you now have a felony on a previously unblemished record. I will suggest to you that in three years you apply to the Office of the Governor and request Restoration of Rights." With tears of joy streaming down my face, I said, "Thank you, your honor, and God bless you." Then I turned toward the prosecuting attorneys and thanked them for the plea offer. They seemed somewhat surprised that I would thank them.

My attorney and I hugged and she reminded me to call her office the next day to make an appointment to come in so we could talk, freely, face to face. This felt surreal to me. I was going home today! Today! I could hardly believe it. I had waited four months for this day to come, and perhaps some part of me wondered if it would ever come. We serve a faithful God, who indeed brings about change, sometimes suddenly when we least expect it, and often when we have just about given up all hope. Psalm 116:1 says, "I love the Lord, for He heard my voice. He heard my cry for mercy and He turned His ear to me. I will call on Him for as long as I live."

As I was being transported back to the jail for out processing I prayed that David and James would be led by the Lord, and know if it was right for them to accept the plea offer when it was presented to the two of them later in the week. I hoped all three of my sons would be told I had accepted the offer that day, and was going home.

When I came into the pod I must have had a smile a mile wide across my face because I had not been in the pod a minute when one of the women looked at me and asked, "Mrs. Smith, are you going home today?" I nodded my head, and happy tears streamed down my face. She squealed, jumped up, and hollered to the women, "Mrs. Smith is going home. Mrs. Smith is going home." Some of the women quickly gathered around me, hugging me, and saying they were happy for me. Lauren looked totally shocked, hugged me, and began to cry. I hugged her and told her she was going to be fine. I told her she should request to be moved into the cell with Fanny, even though Fanny would be leaving in about two weeks. Lauren nodded her head, but the tears continued to flow.

The pod officer instructed me to go to my cell and prepare for "B&B removal shortly." "B&B removal" was a term the jail used, meaning "body and baggage removal." It was the terminology the officers used each time someone was going home. I went up to my cell, opened my tote and removed the things I had already decided

I would leave behind. For a moment I stood in the middle of the cell and prayed, "Lord, may I never, ever come to a place like this, or any kind of jail, as an inmate, ever again. Thank you, Lord, for this wonderful day."

I hoped I'd get to see Fanny, who was still in class, before I left. In less than five minutes I was ready to go. As I came out of my cell, one of the women asked to carry my tote down the steps. I gave my long johns and socks to Lauren, who continued to cry. I quickly passed out a few things that I wanted to give to some of the women. We all said goodbye and many of the women hugged me again and asked me to continue to pray for them. I thanked Officer Blake for her kindness, during the four months I was there. As she escorted me out of the pod many of the women called, "Good bye Mrs. Smith, God bless you. Remember us in your prayers."

As we left the pod, the officer said little but was her usual formal self, entering codes on doors to allow us access through various restricted corridors. Suddenly I said to her, "Officer Blake, would you please say goodbye to my cellmate, Fanny, for me. I had hoped I'd get to say goodbye to her myself, but I guess that won't be possible since she's still in class." Abruptly the officer halted, and without saying a word, buzzed a large door to our right. Stepping inside she said "excuse me" to the teacher behind the desk, then quickly announced, "Smith is leaving." Some of the women jumped up and came rushing toward me cheering and saying, "Oh, Mrs. Smith, we are so happy for you." Bridget picked me up and spun me around. Fanny and I hugged with tears flowing down both of our faces. "Mrs. Smith, you know I will miss you," Fanny said. "And I will certainly miss you, too, Fanny. You've been the best cellmate. Let's keep in touch when you get out." I quickly told her the things I had left behind on her bunk for her, and asked her to look out for Lauren. I thanked the teacher for letting us interrupt his class, and I thanked Officer Blake for her kindness. We quickly moved on through the corridors and toward the Out Processing Section, also known as the Intake Section, the same room I had stood in four months earlier.

When we got to the Out Processing Section, Officer Blake became a bit less formal, smiled, and said, "Smith, now, you take good care of yourself, you hear." "Yes, Officer Blake. Thank you. I will, and you take care of yourself, as well. God bless you." She nodded, turned, and quickly left.

I stood at the clothing window, tote in hand, waiting to return the jail's property. The property officer received the jail's property, and then returned my personal belongings. The clothing I wore the day I came in had been folded up in a storage bin, labeled with my name and the last four of my social security number, unwashed, and wrinkled for the last four months. That would be the clothing I'd be wearing home today. I did not care. They could have given me a sack to wear home and I would have still been smiling from ear to ear.

When the property exchange officer was almost finished with me, I asked her if there was a public phone I could use to call someone to come get me. She directed me to a red phone which she said I would find on the other side of the door. She told me I could only use the red phone when I was completely processed out, and when I actually went through the door. She said once you go through the door you are technically on the outside of the jail, even though you're still in the building, and you cannot come back in through that door, once it closes behind you. I thought to myself, no one who has been in this place, with a sane mind, would even remotely want to come back.

Four months earlier, when I was first arrested, it was my dear friend Debbie whom I had called. Initially it was the only call I had been allowed to make. Once again, Debbie was the person I was calling; this time to ask her to come get me, and silently praying she would be at her desk. Debbie answered right away. Glory to God!! Today this was not a collect call, as all my calls to her had been for the past four months. "Debbie, this is Diana. Can you come get me?" She must have been in shock momentarily at hearing my voice and hearing those words. "Diana?" she said. "Where are you? Are you at the jail? Come get you? What has happened?" "Debbie, I can come home. I was offered a plea agreement today, and I accepted it. I can come home!! Can you come get me and I'll tell you everything when I see you." "Yes, yes, I'll be there in just a few minutes. Are you on the outside of the jail?" "You will see me in the parking lot," I said.

The lightweight navy blue trousers and short sleeved blouse were now several sizes too large, and hung on me like a sack. Unarguably I had lost a substantial amount of weight, at least twenty-five pounds was my guess. I did not care what my clothing looked like. I was focused on the fact that I was going home!! No longer confined, but FREE!!

11

COUNTING THE LOSS

Strangely, I do not remember what the weather was like the day I was released except I know for certain it wasn't raining. There could have been a blizzard and I would not have had one complaint to God about the weather. I was beside myself with joy, to be going home, to be able to see Julia and everyone who had done so much for us during the past four months. Debbie arrived within a short time after I called her, although I thought it would take her much longer, through the rush hour traffic. She squealed when she saw me and we ran toward each other in the parking lot, hugging and laughing. She was bubbling over with questions about how, when, and what had suddenly happened. We both knew the hand of God had intervened, and brought about this change.

On our way out of the jail's parking lot Debbie telephoned Pastor Rebecca. The joy and happiness in Pastor Rebecca's voice were unmistakable. Debbie and Pastor Rebecca reminded me that Sharon had encouraged the congregation to pray and fast for me on the previous Friday night. Pastor Rebecca said this was a direct answer to the prayer and fasting. Debbie called Sharon next and she, too, was delighted to hear the miraculous news of my sudden release. There is no question that intercessory prayer and fasting changes things, people, situations, circumstances, and perhaps even the hand of God.

Debbie and I talked excitedly as we drove along. I related all the details to her and told her the same plea offer would be made available to David and James later in the week. We arrived at the Latimer's home, where Julia was staying. I hoped it would be a wonderful surprise, but somehow the news had gotten there ahead of us. Julia opened the door for us and seemed to be as much in shock at seeing me, as I was at being released. I grabbed her and squeezed her tightly in my arms. I wanted to keep hugging her and looking at her to see if she had changed during the months I had been away. I knew we had all changed, not so much in a physical sense, but I knew none of us would ever be the same people we were four months ago.

We called Sarah, and she and her daughter came right away to the Latimer's home. We called Madeline, and then Joanna, although she was still out of the country. Everyone was delighted, laughing, crying, and saying God had certainly, finally intervened on my behalf.

That night Julia and I slept together in the guest room, in the twin size bed that she usually slept in. I'm certain I must have disturbed her because I tossed and turned endlessly during the night. I kept waking up, sitting up abruptly and looking around the room to be certain I was not at the jail. I kept praying, and thanking my Father for His loving kindness and His intervention on my behalf. I asked Him to please, extend that same loving kindness and mercy to David and James for their release. It seemed I had not slept in a real bed in an eternity.

On Tuesday morning I got up at 5:30 a.m., when Julia and the Latimer's daughter, Carly, got up for school. Carly and Julia drove to school each morning so I had them drop me off at my house, on their way to school. I stayed there all day, walking through each room, again and again, praying, looking at things, especially family pictures, as if seeing everything for the first time. I continuously prayed out loud for each of my children.

I agonized again, remembering that by my actions and decisions to help Matt, I had put all of us in a serious legal situation. I thanked my Father that He is the God of another chance, even when we don't deserve another chance.

There were so many wonderful memories in our house, memories of gatherings with friends and family, birthdays and special holiday celebrations, teenage girl sleepovers, prayer meetings, and neighbors dropping in to chat. There were also some not so pleasant memories in this house; such as that night in October, 2003, when the police and detectives came looking for Matt, and when they came again in early May, 2004 with the extensive search warrant and found the $50,000 in my attic, which I had put there, and which belonged to Matt.

It was still our house and for that I was thankful to God, beyond words, for a place to come back to. Some of the women whom I had met during the time I was incarcerated, left the jail saying they had no family and no place to go, except perhaps to the homeless shelter. During the months I was away God had continuously been so gracious and kind, making sure the mortgage was paid so we would have a house to come back to.

Maybe it would be hard to face some people in light of what had happened in our family, in this small community. I knew some would probably no longer want to be associated with me or my family, and would eagerly point the finger of criticism. I would determine in my heart to forgive them, in advance, and to pray that they would never be in such a position that involved one of their children or someone they loved. When we think about it, the playing field is level for all of us at the foot of the cross. Romans 3:23 says, "For all have sinned and fallen short." No one can really point the finger of criticism at another, since all of us have something in our lives that has humiliated, embarrassed, or ashamed us, so much so that we'd like to pretend it never happened.

I purposed and determined in my heart that I would not leave the area, sell my house or move, but I would continue to live here, and by the grace and mercy of God I would hold my head up and go forward, knowing God had forgiven me. I would not allow the past to hold me back like a restraining order on my life.

When all of this began, months earlier, I wanted to run to the farthest corner of the earth and hide. I wanted to go to sleep and wake up to find out it had all been an extremely bad dream, a nightmare in fact. Since I could do neither of those things, I continued to go to the One whom I always run to. His Word says in Psalms 32:7 that He is my hiding place. Daily I would "hide" myself in His Word, in prayer, in repentance, in brokenness. I knew beyond a doubt that no medication, no sedative, no drug, no alcohol, nothing, could bring about the healing that I so desperately needed. He was the only One who could reach into the depth of my soul and touch me where I ached and the pain didn't seem to want to go away.

It goes without saying that many people's lives were affected by the decisions Matt, Chris and Sean made on that night in June, 2003, which lead to the senseless death of the eighteen year old young man. My heart broke for the family's irreplaceable loss. I wished I could have talked to them and told them how sorry I was for their great loss. I would have asked them to please forgive my son, and the other two young men. I prayed for them.

Now, my family was about to experience loss, even more than we already had, since the recommendation of the prosecuting attorneys was going to be that Matt be given two life sentences. That was far more than any of us could have imagined. Matt would be formally sentenced sometime around mid-October. And David, oh God! David was now charged with the same charges as Matt. These things spoke of great loss to me. James had been incarcerated twice because of this situation and in all probability would not be rehired back at his job. He had been one semester away from obtaining his Associates Degree when he was arrested the first time. Would he now have the desire to continue with his education? There was also the loss that David, Chris and Sean's families would experience should they go to prison. David and Chris each had two small children. Who could begin to calculate the loss of being a part of their children's lives? Matt's friends, Rick and Cathy, had lost their first baby since this ordeal began. Julia had celebrated her sixteenth birthday with none of us around, and lost her virginity during the four months I was away from her. What about Joanna, and the trauma for her as well? So much had been lost, and some of it would never be regained. We now had to await David's fate because of the list of numerous charges the prosecutors decided to charge him with.

The plan for Tuesday evening, my second night free, was that Julia and I would spend the night at Sarah's home and the utilities would be turned back on at our house on Wednesday morning. Julia and I would begin staying at our house again, after that. The young couple at church who had been using my car for the last four months would return it to me by the end of the week. I was thankful that no restrictions had been placed on me by the court, such as driving restrictions, or probation, although I had been given substantial court fines, in addition to owing my attorney for her legal representation. Although I now had a felony, I didn't allow myself to give a lot of thought to what that meant in actuality, such as the loss of one's Civil Rights, mainly the loss of the right to vote. As time passed and I had time to think more about what it meant to have a felony, I realized just how precious and fragile our rights are.

Debbie left her cell phone with me for the day, in order for me to be able to make any phone calls I needed to make. Of highest priority was the phone call I needed to make to Ms. O'Hara, to make an appointment with her. I wanted to thank her again for all she had done, and all she had tried to do. In addition, there was the dreaded issue which I knew I would have to discuss with her, about the remainder of Matt's money, which I believed was still buried on our property, and the detectives still suspected.

As urgently as I needed our home phone turned back on, I decided I would not have it turned back on for a few weeks. There were several reasons for my decision. Since our phone had been wire tapped prior to me going to jail, I didn't want it back on yet. While I was going through some of the mail that had been boxed up and saved for me, I found our most recent phone bill. The amount due was over five hundred dollars. Matt had called Lauren collect, from jail, sometimes as much as ten times a day when she was staying temporarily at my house.

The next high priority call I needed to make was to my supervisor at work to talk to her about my job. After speaking with her I was disappointed, but not surprised, to hear they would not be taking me back as an employee, since I now had a felony. With God's help I would find work.

That evening Julia and I had dinner at Sarah's house and spent the night. Sarah made spaghetti and a delicious salad. I'm certain I ate like someone who was starving. I had two helpings of everything, and kept telling her how delicious the meal was. A friend from church called Sarah's house to tell us that our local newspaper had run a front page article saying I had accepted a plea offer and had been released. I wondered for the hundredth time if Matt would ever fully understand what our family and so many others had been through.

Bright and early on Wednesday morning I was up and dressed. By the time Sarah was ready to leave for work I had her to drop me off at my house. Utilities were turned back on that day. In addition to continuing to pray, I busied myself cleaning out the refrigerator and doing some other chores. Sarah left her cell phone with me to make any calls I needed to make. Later in the day I had an appointment to go to Mrs. O'Hara's office. Pastor Rebecca came that morning and talked and prayed with me. I was delighted to see her. Several other friends from church visited and prayed with me. I asked them to pray for me to have the courage to tell Mrs. O'Hara what the detectives already suspected. On Monday in court when I had accepted the plea offer, Mrs. O'Hara whispered to me that I was still going to be watched, because the detectives suspected Matt still had money on our property, buried someplace. They were right.

The sad thing for me was I knew that in revealing what was most probably still buried on the property, I would have to betray Matt's confidence. Matt sent word to me through several people, when I was in jail, that he did not want me to reveal what he had on our property, or he would not forgive me. I knew he would be extremely angry, but he had to know what we had been through, individually, and as a family because of him, and because of my

decision to help him. As much as his words stung about not forgiving me if I revealed the money he had on our property, and as
much as I hated to betray his confidence, I knew I had to do what
the Lord had already put in my heart to do. I felt the Holy Spirit
was saying to me, "Do what you know in your heart is the right
thing to do and I will protect you. Just do what you know in your
heart is the right thing to do." I had to be obedient to God, first
and foremost.

Whatever money was buried on the property did not belong
to me, nor did it belong to anyone who lived in my house, because Matt did not live at my house. Since the detectives still
suspected there was money on our property and were going to
continue watching us, I knew they would also periodically come
to my home, with search warrants, whenever they felt like it, until they had it. I did not want to live like that, having to look over
my shoulders and having my life entwined in lies, to cover what
Matt had put on the property, thereby putting all of us again in
great jeopardy, and certainly at risk for going back to jail. How
ridiculous that would have been! How foolish! No amount of
money is ever worth giving up one's freedom. I had to do what
was right in God's sight, because He is the One that I stand an-
swerable to.

I have always been an advocate for my children, when they
were younger, and throughout the years; always there for them,
always going to bat for them if I felt someone had mistreated
them or wronged them in any way. This time I knew I could not
be a proponent for Matt's cause, because the safety of this family
and my own peace of mind far outweighed what Matt wanted.
I did not know how much was buried in the backyard, but with
him forbidding me to reveal what he had buried, I knew there
was apparently something of significance there, or he would not

have sent such a stern message to me, through different people, several different times. Matt trusted me, and I had never betrayed his trust. It saddened me greatly to have to do what I knew I had to do.

12

WHAT WAS HIDDEN, NOW REVEALED

Ms. O'Hara's office scheduled me for a 5:00 p.m. appointment and as the last client for the day. I chatted with Allison, while waiting, and thanked her for everything they tried to do for me while I was incarcerated. Finally, Ms. O'Hara was ready for me. We talked about the four months I spent in jail. She said she was still angry with Matt for dragging our family into a mess he created. She felt the ordeal had taken quite a toll on all of us and had aged me. She was right. The stress in my face was obvious to everyone who knew me, and didn't seem to go away, even with a good night's sleep. My once natural jet black hair was now bursting with silver streaks that appeared almost overnight and seemed to grow greatly in number every day.

As we talked I brought up the subject of paying her and as always she was gracious saying she knew I would, when I had it. She reiterated that the detectives still believed there was money on my property and I could expect we were going to continue to be watched until they turned up the money they were pretty sure was "out there," somewhere on our property. She said they would continue to come with a search warrant whenever they wanted to and disrupt my life, home, sanity and peace of mine. I took a deep breath and told her, "the detectives are probably right, Ms. O'Hara. To the best of my knowledge there *is* still money buried on my property." She did not look surprised, but waited for me to continue. I told her that over a year earlier, in the summer of 2003, I had come home one day to find Matt at the house, in the back yard digging, or more accurately, covering a hole he had already dug. I walked to where he was in the yard and asked him what he was doing. He stumbled through his words for a moment, but finally told me he had buried some money there, in the yard. When I questioned him more extensively about why he wasn't putting it in the bank he said he wasn't comfortable with doing that, and he had no place else to put it. The more I questioned him, the more evasive he became, and the more I realized he was probably into something he had no business to be involved in. I told him that day that I wanted it taken out of my yard. Sometime later he told me he had moved it. Months later, before he left the state and went on the run from the police, he called and told me the money was still on the property.

I told Ms. O'Hara that while I had been incarcerated Matt had sent several messages through various people that I was not, under any circumstances, to reveal the money he had buried in my yard. Even in the three days I had been home, he had sent the same message through two different people, saying he would not forgive me if I revealed where his money was. I told her I did not want it on my property. She asked me if I wanted her to call the detectives and tell them while I was still there in her office. I said yes.

She made the call. We asked them to please come to my home the next day, in an unmarked car, if possible. I didn't wish to draw the attention of my neighbors any more than we already had. I asked Ms. O'Hara what she thought would happen to me. Did she think I would have to go back to jail for revealing the money? She said she didn't think any further charges would be brought against me and that I should expect the detectives the next morning. We would talk again after the detectives left my house on Thursday. I thanked her, hugged her, and left her office.

Sarah was going to be home from work on Thursday morning, so I asked her to come get me when the detectives came. I did not want to be at the house while they were in my yard, digging for the money.

Without a doubt I felt badly that I had to betray Matt's confidence, but simultaneously I felt an enormous weight had been lifted from me. There was a huge sense of relief, and peace that I had made the right decision. I knew my decision would not be popular with all of my family but I vowed to have no regrets about that decision.

Around 10:00 a.m., on Thursday morning Detectives Ellis and Jefferson arrived, in an unmarked car, as requested. I immediately went outside to meet them and walked them to the place in the backyard I had seen Matt covering the hole, in the summer of 2003. Sarah arrived within minutes of the detectives' arrival. She and I left the house and stayed away all day.

When we returned, late that evening, they were gone, and I didn't know if I had put them on a wild goose chase or if they had actually found the money. Sarah and I walked to the particular place in the backyard where I had directed them. There was evidence that some fairly serious digging had taken place, but we had no way of knowing if they'd found anything. It was too late in the day to call my attorney to ask if the detectives called her. I decided I would give her office a call the next morning.

On Friday morning, when I called Ms. O'Hara's office, Allison excitedly asked me to hold while she got Ms. O'Hara. Ms. O'Hara sounded almost as excited as Allison. "Well, did they find anything yesterday or was it a wild goose case?" I began. "Wow, Diana, did they ever find something! They found $200,000, neatly wrapped and packed in a large plastic container. It was several feet down in the ground, under concrete. Matt was very thorough." Ms. O'Hara continued. "Diana, I cannot begin to tell you how happy I am that you took this courageous step. I know how hard it must have been for you to betray Matt's confidence; but we both know there are people who will take someone's life for far less than $200,000 and if word had somehow gotten out on the street, about the amount of money buried on your property, none of you would have been safe." I totally agreed with her, and breathed a deep sigh of relief knowing there was nothing left of the money, not on the property, nor anywhere else.

Mrs. O'Hara went on to say the detectives had taken pictures of the money they dug it up, and made a caption that read, "You have your mother to thank for this." They took the picture to the jail and showed Matt. For Matt it was like rubbing salt into a wound. Needless to say, he was furious with me. I would not allow myself to become upset or worry about the fact that he was angry with me. I put him in God's most capable hands. I knew Ms. O'Hara was right; none of us would have been safe, if word of that money had gotten out on the streets. It was headline news in our local newspaper on Friday morning.

I was surprised at the number of people who knew me, including Christians, family members and close friends who asked me why I had revealed the money to the police, and why hadn't I just kept a little for myself, with all the bills I certainly must have. I told them why. It was not mine to keep. I wanted to be able to sleep at night, to look at myself in the mirror every day, and know I didn't take anything, from anyone, that I did not work for, or earn, honestly. I did not ever want to begin to rely on someone else's money as my source. My "Source" has always been Jesus Christ, the One who truly provides well for His children. Proverbs 10:22 says, "The blessing of the Lord brings wealth, and He adds no trouble to it." That was the kind of blessing I wanted; one that came from the Lord and added no trouble to it.

On Friday, four days after I came home, I got a call from Ms. O'Hara letting me know that David and James were offered the same plea offer I had taken on Monday. James accepted the plea offer and would be coming home that day, but David turned it down. After I had accepted the plea offer, I had second thoughts about whether or not David and James should accept it because it had the stipulation of that unwanted felony attached to it. In my opinion David and James had done nothing wrong. James had gone to New Jersey and brought back Matt's clothing and luggage after Matt had been apprehended in that area and extradited back to our state. Unknown to James, the luggage had a hidden lining, at the bottom, which concealed $12,000 in cash. I was the one who opened that luggage and took out the money, at Matt's request. Also, I initially felt David did the right thing to turn down the plea offer. As far as I was concerned David, like James, had done nothing wrong and was propelled into the situation because of being related to Matt, and because he was a part of the phone calls from Matt at the jail. All of us were a part of those calls. Hence the reason we all received the conspiracy charges.

Sarah picked James up from the jail when he was released that Friday afternoon, and although I was absolutely delighted to see him, I asked him why he accepted the plea offer. "James, you didn't do anything wrong. Why did you accept the plea offer?"

"Mom, you and I both know that if I rejected their offer and the case went to trial I would not get a fair trial in this area." "But James, you didn't do anything wrong or illegal." "That might be true Mom, but the prosecutors don't care about that. They consider all of us guilty." "You may be right James, but I think David was right to turn the offer down, although I am glad it was made available to each of us." Again, that was my initial reaction, until I saw the devastating results, several weeks later, of David turning down the plea offer.

More than two weeks after I was released from jail, Matt's formal sentencing was scheduled, and although I had not been allowed to attend his trial in July, there were no restrictions on me now, and I knew, God willing, I would be at his sentencing. I knew also that he would certainly still be angry with me for revealing the money.

On October 15, 2004, the morning of Matt's sentencing, I sat in Circuit Court dressed in a dark suit. I sat quietly between James, Paul, Mr. Harvey, and his assistant Sam Jones. Paul had known Matt since high school. Silently I prayed the same prayer I had been praying for months, that Matt would not be given such a severe sentence, as had been recommended. We sat reading or whispering quietly until Matt's case was called. Detectives Jefferson and Ellis sat on the opposite side of the courtroom, in the rear.

A few minutes later Matt was escorted into the courtroom and the first thing I noticed about him was that he was indeed, extremely thin. I groaned when I saw him. I knew all the stress of the past sixteen months had taken a toll on him, just as it had the rest of us. It had been about five months since I'd seen him. In October, 2003, a little over a year earlier and before he went on the run from the police, he weighed about 180 pounds at five feet, eleven inches. Now, one year later, he could not have been more than 130 pounds. He was neatly dressed in light khaki colored trousers and a soft blue long sleeved shirt. His skin was clear, and although he didn't look ill, he was much too thin for his height. We were all seated directly behind him. As he was being seated, Mr. Harvey left us and joined Matt. Matt turned and nodded his head to James, Paul and Mr. Jones, but he did not even look at me. Paul put his arm around my shoulder and said, "It's okay, Mrs. Smith. He's still angry with you right now, but he'll get over it. Give him a while."

Normally there is only one bailiff covering the courtroom, but today there were two. Suddenly a SWAT team entered the courtroom from several different doors, and began taking positions in various places around the courtroom with weapons clearly visible. One of them took a position at the door leading into the courtroom and no one else was allowed in. One of the SWAT team members came and stood directly behind Matt. "What is the point of this?" I quietly asked out loud to those around me. "Do they think he will try to escape? How overly dramatic can this court be?!"

A female reporter from the local newspaper sat quietly in the back of the courtroom, near Detectives Jefferson and Ellis, periodically leaning over to ask them a question.

Matt sat quietly next to Mr. Harvey. Occasionally he turned and looked at the detectives with a smirk on his face that I didn't like seeing come from him. The judge made preliminary comments and then asked one of the prosecutors to speak. It all seemed like a mere formality. In that moment I had an epiphany. I felt certain the decision had already been made for Matt, and the judge and prosecutors already knew what they were going to do. There wasn't going to be any leniency or mercy shown here, today, to my son. I could already see that. One of the prosecutors began to speak, telling the judge why, in his opinion, Matt should be given the maximum sentence. Then Mr. Harvey spoke, telling the judge why, in his opinion, Matt should not be given the maximum sentence.

Mr. Harvey had spoken to me before we entered the courtroom asking if there was anything noteworthy which Matt had done that would make the judge not just look at him as a murderer. I immediately remembered the time two years earlier, when Matt and his girlfriend witnessed a State Trooper in a high speed chase, crash his cruiser into a telephone pole near a busy intersection. Matt was the first person to come to the aid of the State Trooper. Thinking the officer's smoking cruiser might burst into flames he approached the semi-conscious officer and said, "Officer, you have been hurt and your vehicle is smoking. May I lift you out of the vehicle and onto the ground?" The officer told him yes. Matt gently lifted him out, as a crowd gathered around. In less than five minutes swarms of police, a helicopter, an ambulance, and fire trucks converged on the area to come to the aid of the injured trooper. Matt stepped back into the crowd quietly, until one of the policemen on the scene demanded to know, "Who removed this officer from his cruiser?" Matt then stepped forward giving his name, address, driver's license, and phone number. No one ever called our home to thank Matt, not even the injured officer, when he recovered. Mr. Harvey told that story in court and the judge, looking somewhat surprised, glanced at the prosecutors as if to say, "Hey, did you guys know about that?" Matt's girlfriend had related the details of that incident to me when it occurred.

When Mr. Harvey finished speaking the judge asked Matt if he had anything to say, before she pronounced his sentence. Surprisingly, he said yes. He stood up, cleared his throat, and began speaking. "Your Honor," he began, "Thank you for allowing me a few minutes to speak. I'd like the court to know that I feel the detectives in charge of our case and the prosecutors are a bunch of liars. When the detectives came to my mother's home in May they told her they would notify her or her attorney when the warrants were issued, and she would be able to turn herself in. They did not do that. Instead they waited until her attorney left town on Memorial Day weekend, and arrested her in her office. That was totally unnecessary." His words brought stinging accusations against the detectives and prosecutors. One of the prosecutors quickly spoke up, objecting to Matt calling them a bunch of liars. The judge cleared her throat and made some comments to Matt about being tactful in his remarks. Matt nodded his head and continued speaking. "As I was saying, the detectives and prosecutors are a bunch of liars." The prosecutors objected a second time, and this time the judge directed her comments to Mr. Harvey asking him to please instruct his client on what is acceptable decorum in the courtroom. Mr. Harvey whispered briefly to Matt, who had unquestionably made his point. Everyone in the courtroom knew he was right. I wanted to hug Matt for having the courage to speak what was in his heart. They were a bunch of liars!!

Matt continued his comments, "Your Honor, the detectives have always known that whatever I was doing, my mother and my family were not in any way involved. They chose to use my family as scapegoats to get to me because I refused to cooperate, to name names, or to accept their plea offers." He paused then said, "Your Honor, I received a letter from my mother recently, and in closing I would like to read a brief portion from that letter, if I may." The judge nodded her head, and gave me a peculiar look. I had no idea what part of that long letter Matt was going to read, or why he felt it necessary to read it, but I braced myself for whatever was about to come forth. The letter had been written to him a week earlier. In the letter I talked to him about how he was raised to know right from wrong, about the choices we each make in life, and how sometimes the consequences of those choices follow us to the grave because they become the watershed turns in our lives and cannot be undone. I had also addressed his anger toward me, for revealing the buried money. In the letter I said, "You are angry with me for revealing money you buried on our property without my permission; so tell me Matt, who really has the right to be angry? Look at all the lives that have been affected by your lifestyle decisions. Look at the people in our family who have each paid a severe price for what we did to help you. Then tell me, if you will, who truly has the right to be angry?!" If anyone has the right to be angry, isn't it the rest of us?"

I lowered my head as Matt began reading. He began reading where I had spoken to him about how he had been raised, and how God had given him numerous opportunities to get his life right. As he read, I momentarily looked up at the judge's face, and for a split second I thought I saw a mother, like myself, who felt compassion for a young man who had made some terrible decisions. Matt concluded the reading of the letter by saying, "Your Honor, I want you to know that I was raised in a good Christian home, and raised to know right from wrong, although I have made some regrettable choices in my life. Thank you, Your Honor, for allowing me to speak." He quietly sat down next to Mr. Harvey. I wanted to tell him I loved him very much, and nothing he had done would change that. God shows His children unconditional love, no matter how we mess up in life.

Whatever I had seen briefly in the judge's face, in the way of compassion, was gone. She hesitated for a moment, shuffled some papers that were in front of her and then clearing her throat and speaking in a voice as cold as ice water she said, "Thank you, Mr.

Smith. Have you anything further to say before I pronounce your sentence?" "No, Your Honor, nothing further, thank you." This time he turned briefly to me, for the first time, smiled his "I love you, Mom" smile, and winked at me. My eyes filled with tears, as I smiled back at him. "Very well, then, Mr. Smith. Please stand as I read your sentence." As Matt and Mr. Harvey stood, tears flowed like a stream down my face even before she began reading the sentence.

"Mr. Smith," she began, "you were indicted by a grand jury, and found guilty by a jury, on the charges of First Degree Murder, Burglary While Armed, Use of A Firearm in the Commission of a Felony by a previously convicted felon, and Conspiracy to Commit Capital Murder, or murder for hire..." and the list went on. With no expression on her face and even less emotion in her voice she continued. "This court has found you guilty of the charges and sentences you to two life sentences, plus thirty-three years. Mr. Smith, I remand you to the custody of the court."

As the two bailiffs approached Matt to take him away, I stood. "Your Honor, I request permission to hug my son." "I beg your pardon?" She asked dryly. I repeated, "I request permission to hug my son." Her reply was swift, direct and emotionless. "No, I cannot allow that. Please remove Mr. Smith from the courtroom." Mr. Harvey walked over to me and put his arms around me for a moment. Matt turned briefly one last time, before being escorted out of the courtroom. "It's okay Mom, please don't cry. You know that justice isn't just; certainly not in this court of law, and certainly not in this county." James walked out of the courtroom.

There was no question in my mind that justice wasn't just, not in this courtroom, not in this county, and far too many times not in these great United States of America, where African American men and other minorities are involved. How could justice be just when my son had just been given two life sentences, plus thirty-three years? The other two co-defendants, Sean and Chris, who were not African American, had accepted the plea bargains offered to them and would each receive about five years, when by their own admission all of them participated in the crime. David, who wasn't even with them, was potentially looking at getting more time than Sean and Chris combined. Where was the justice or fairness to this kind of sentencing?! Wasn't it really because my sons were African American and Sean and Chris were not? How could anyone think otherwise? Unless we live under a rock we have all seen this kind of lopsided justice which has existed from the time of slavery, where far too much sentencing time is given for the crimes of African Americans, and sadly it continues to happen. It is a fact that a disproportionately larger number of minorities fill the prisons because the pendulum does not swing in favor of minorities in many courtrooms in our country. When will we see this change in our country?

I could have understood if my son had been given twenty years, allowed to be eligible for parole, and asked to make restitution to the family who lost their son. I would have understood that; but nothing in me could understand two life sentences for a murder that was not premeditated. We are supposed to be a civilized society and yet we "warehouse" people in prisons, give them ridiculous sentences, and many times take away all hope of them ever returning to society.

13

DAVID'S TRIAL AND SENTENCING

Every week I went to the jail to visit with David, who remained in general population. David's trial and formal sentencing were scheduled for the spring of 2005. Beatrice visited David only once during the entire time of his incarceration, even when he was taken from jail to prison.

We were no longer allowed to visit or write Matt after he was formally sentenced, while he remained at the jail, since the prosecutors asked the judge to suspend all of Matt's jail privileges until Department of Corrections (DOC) took him to prison. Those privileges included his right to have visitors, his right to send or receive mail, and his right to make phone calls. Additionally, the prosecutors requested that Matt remain in isolation and confinement until DOC came for him, whenever that might be. They felt Matt still might have an influence on people outside the walls of the jail, and could ask someone to do something illegal. Matt would only be allowed visits from his legal counsel or any clergy who wished to visit him. He would be allowed to receive legal mail only, from the court or his attorney. He would be allowed to call his attorney only when he put in a written request to the jail, and the request would have to be pre-approved before he would be allowed to make the call.

Several months earlier in August, 2004 when David's bond was revoked, his attorney asked to be removed from the case, and David was given Mr. Patrick, a court appointed attorney. On the day that James and David were offered the plea agreement David turned it down. I found out later that David went against the advice of Mr. Patrick. Therefore his charges for the money laundering and conspiracy would be scheduled for trial by jury. A second plea offer was also prepared for him because of the second set of much more serious charges which he had received for refusing to testify against Matt. If found guilty of those charges, David was potentially looking at getting the same kind of sentence Matt had been given. When Mr. Patrick read the list of additional charges to me, that David had been given, I thought I would faint. I cried, and I cried out to God. I asked, "Lord, is it not enough that Matt has already been given two life sentences?! Why is this happening to David, who wasn't even at the scene of the crime?"

I went to see David to talk to him and convince him that he definitely needed to accept the second plea offer, given the kind of sentence that was ahead for him if he did not. He was adamant that he was not going to accept any plea offers because he hadn't done anything wrong.

Mr. Patrick was strongly urging David to accept the second plea offer for all the new charges since he had turned down the previous plea offer for the conspiracy charges. I prayed and fasted for God's wisdom in the words I would speak to David. I begged and pleaded with him through tears, telling him if he couldn't do it for himself, then he must think about his two small sons. His children were three and five years old. If he did not accept the second plea offer and his case went to trial, even if he got fifteen years, obviously his sons would grow up without him in their lives. I begged him to pray and seek the wisdom of God so he would make the best decision, with his children in the forefront of his mind. He promised me he would pray about it. I continued to fast and pray for him to make the right choice.

Several days later I went to see him again and he had made the decision to accept the prosecutor's second plea offer for the second group of charges. I was happy to hear that and so was his attorney because he was no longer looking at the possibility of getting a life sentence. I remembered James' words from several weeks earlier that none of us would get a fair trial in this area. In hindsight, I knew he was right.

On the day of David's trial, James, Beatrice and I were in court for him. On the conspiracy and money laundering charges, which he refused a plea offer, he received seven years. For the additional charges, which he accepted the second plea offer he also received seven years. The judge ruled that the two seven year sentences would run concurrently! The blessing was that he did not receive a life sentence, and that he would be serving both sentences at the same time. Still, my heart was filled with pain for him, for Beatrice and for his two small sons. I wept bitter, sad tears every time I thought of what this sentence would mean for David and his family. He was scheduled for formal sentencing several months later.

On the morning of David's formal sentencing, in the spring of 2005, I arrived a few minutes earlier and gave the bailiff a white shirt and suit trousers for David to wear in court, so he didn't have to stand before the judge in the jail's clothing. Beatrice, Madeline and I sat together, hand in hand, directly behind David, who was seated next to Mr. Patrick. James had to work that day and was unable to get off. Madeline had driven over two hours to be with us. I was immensely thankful for her support and friendship.

Although David's sentence was not as harsh as Matt's, still I knew David did not deserve the sentence he received. We all felt the prosecutors were trying to make an example of him, to say, "If you don't cooperate with us, this is what we can do to you and your family." David sat beside his attorney handsome and composed. There seemed to be a peace radiating from him that said, "No matter what happens, I know God is with me, and with God's help I'm going to get through this."

Before pronouncing sentence this judge gave David an opportunity to speak, just as Judge Mayfield had given Matt, several months earlier at his sentencing. David thanked the judge for allowing him a few minutes to speak. Then in a calm and composed voice, he turned toward the three of us and directed his comments first to Beatrice and then to me, asking each of us to forgive him for what he felt he had put us through. Tears streamed down my face, as I responded out loud to him, "You do not owe me an apology. I owe you an apology."

When David finished speaking he turned to the judge and thanked him again. The judge read all the charges beginning with the conspiracy and money laundering charges, and ending with the additional charges, and then he announced that the two seven year sentences would run concurrently. For that I was thankful beyond words! The judge was kind to us and allowed Beatrice, Madeline and me to hug David briefly before he was taken out of the courtroom, unlike Judge Mayfield for Matt's case. I now had two sons going to prison. I could not stop the tears from falling. Madeline and I left the courtroom still in tears. Beatrice lingered behind in the courtroom to speak with David's attorney.

Beatrice caught up to us in the parking lot. She expressed her disappointment and anger with David for turning down the first plea offer, for the conspiracy and money laundering charges, and the result was one of those seven year sentences. I hugged her and told her no decision which had been made could now be undone. We had each made what we felt was the best decision, at the time we made those decisions. I asked her to please stay in touch with me. She told me she would. I encouraged her to use the time ahead of her as a time to better herself educationally so she would not be dependent on anyone. She promised me she was going to do that.

I continued to visit David weekly and he seemed to be at peace with whatever lay ahead for him. Sadly, Matt remained in isolation and confinement. Matt's attorney, my pastor and several other pastors went in to see him often, and the report was always the same. "He is extremely thin, but his mind is sharp and alert. He says the food is terrible, and the portions are meager." I could certainly attest to the fact that the food was disgusting and the portions adequate only for a child.

Daily I prayed for God's hands to be on Matt and David, to protect and sustain them in every way, because I knew the journey ahead of them would be long and certainly not easy. Mr. Harvey told me the jail would not even allow Matt to attend the jail's Sunday church services. He was allowed out of his cell twice a week, to take a shower. His human rights were being violated, in my opinion, although Matt's attorney said the court was not violating any law in their treatment of Matt. I sent a letter to several of our elected officials and even to my congressman to tell them about the food at the jail, Matt's tremendous loss of weight, being kept in isolation continuously, and not being able to have mail, make phone calls, or have family and friends visit him. Some of my elected officials made phone calls and wrote letters to the superintendent of the jail, but the letters and phone calls were ignored and nothing was done. I contacted our local chapter of the NAACP and spoke with its president. He, too, was sympathetic and made several calls to the superintendent of the jail, but nothing changed Matt's situation. Mr. Harvey said Matt was not being abused physically, although he had lost over fifty pounds in less than a year. I felt the only thing sustaining Matt was the prayers that many of us were praying on his behalf.

Several weeks after David's sentencing I began to suspect that not only was Beatrice angry with him, but she was also angry with me. I did not hear from her for weeks and she was not returning my calls. She was not visiting David. I had been much too preoccupied with everything that was still going on with Matt and David's cases to realize Beatrice and I needed to sit down and talk, face to face. Beatrice had always been just as outspoken as I, so I wrongly assumed if she needed to talk to me about anything, she would do so.

Long before David's sentencing Beatrice made a point of telling me, David and others, that if David had to go to away for any extended period of time, she would not wait for him, but would go on with her life. She held true to those words.

Months passed and still I did not hear from Beatrice. Finally, one Friday night I was able to reach her. She had been drinking, and for her it was a good time to get out all the hurt and anger. She spared no words in telling me she felt it was my fault that David went to jail, and although I was hurt by her words, I understood her feelings. At first I wanted to react, and tell her I was disappointed in her, and angry too, that she obviously had no intention of waiting for David. However, I tried to listen to her without defending myself or interrupting. When she had made her point and was finished, she slammed the phone down, without allowing me to say anything. I was hurt and angry now, too, so I prayed.

The Holy Spirit would not allow me to stay angry with Beatrice. Not only was she experiencing the loss of David in their family, and the income he provided, but she had lost her job and their apartment. She moved back home with her parents until she was able to manage the financial load that suddenly became hers alone to take care of. There was understandably a monumental amount of hurt, pain, and anger that she was trying to deal with. I needed to be praying fervently for her. I began praying every day for her and my grandsons, although it would be several years before I would see or hear from her again.

14

D.O.C. FINALLY COMES

The weeks and months that followed Matt's and David's formal sentencings were a blur. I was a walking shock trauma victim. Although I was functioning and taking care of the daily tasks of managing my household, and a new job, still I felt like Humpty-Dumpty, who had a tremendous fall from the wall, and nothing had been put back together again, as it was before. I was easily teary eyed, and extremely sensitive. Particular words triggered an involuntary response of tears from me. If someone asked, "How are your sons, Diana?" They needed to be prepared for tears first, and a verbal response later. For those who knew me, no explanation was necessary. For those who did not know me, no amount of explaining would have sufficed. The difficulty for me was interacting with people outside of my circle of close friends and family, and hearing other people talk about their children, or ask questions about mine, especially in my new work place environment. My personality changed dramatically. I was no longer the outgoing, happy, friendly person whom I had always been. There was so much pain and brokenness in me that for a season I become reclusive and introverted.

The holidays approached and I declined all invitations from family and friends. I could not be cheerful during the holidays and I didn't want my sadness to cause others to be uncomfortable.

The best thing that happened during December was that Joanna returned home on Christmas day from her trip abroad, after seven months of being away. James, Julia, Joanna and I spent the day exclusively together. It was the best day I had since coming home. I cooked some of each of their favorite foods. We talked about Joanna's trip and looked at lots of lovely pictures. Still, I missed Matt and David more than words could express, and there was an ache in my heart and soul that only God could understand or fill, and the tears came when I least expected them to come.

"Mom, you're so thin, but you look wonderful," Joanna said. "You look wonderful, too, Joanna." She was tanned and just as beautiful as she'd always been. She seemed wiser and more mature. There was a special glow to her face that a woman gets when she is in love. Joanna had met and gotten to know a young man while she was away.

Joanna stared deeply into my eyes and seemed to be searching to be sure I was the same Mom she had left. I don't know if she could see it then, but the circumstances and the toll of the past year had unquestionably changed me, sometimes beyond my own self recognition. I knew I would never be the same person I was seven months ago. None of us would. How could we be?

In spite of the fact that we would not have Matt, David or either of my two precious grandsons with us for Christmas, I truly thanked God for the three children I did have with me. It was a quiet Christmas holiday, unlike any other we had experienced. There were sad and happy moments that day.

In the days following Joanna's return, she wanted to know more of the details of what had transpired. James, Julia and I each told her from our personal perspectives. Sometimes in trying to answer some of her questions my feelings and thoughts were almost inexpressible, and I became so emotional and weepy that I could not verbally respond for a few minutes.

One day as I was cleaning the kitchen the magnitude of all that had happened swept over me like an enormous tidal wave. I slid down on the floor, drew my knees up to my chest, and cried uncontrollably for twenty minutes. Julia knelt beside me, put her arms around me, and held me until I stopped crying.

Aside from what I was still experiencing emotionally, one thing was clear to me, beyond a shadow of doubt; had I not been a born again child of God with Him sustaining me and holding me, someone would have had to commit me to a hospital. However, the saving grace that got me through each day, each moment, was the fact that I made time, daily, to go into the presence of God and take in large dosages of His Word. In the process of daily survival I continued to fast often. Without God's unconditional love and help, I would not have made the effort to get out of bed. I held on to the Lord, my God, and His Word, with the tenacity of a pit bull. There were days when I wondered if I would ever stop crying, and if this incredible pain in my heart would go away. I could not explain why I had managed my emotions better when I was at the jail for four months than I was managing since I came home.

Several months after David and Matt's formal sentencings I spoke with each of their attorneys, asking them when DOC would come to transport Matt and David to the prisons where they would be housed. Mr. Harvey said he didn't know why DOC hadn't come for Matt, since he had been formally sentenced over eight months earlier. He promised he would look into it for me. He said Matt would certainly do much better once he was taken from the county jail, because when he got to prison he would then be allowed to receive and send mail, and of course to have visitors.

Mr. Harvey called me a couple days later to tell me he had spoken to DOC and was told they hadn't come for Matt because they had not received the required, formal sentencing order, signed by the Circuit Court judge. Mr. Harvey said he didn't understand why the formal sentencing order had not been sent to DOC months earlier. I decided to make some phone calls since Mr. Harvey was not having any success in finding out where the signed order was. I called the office of the prosecutors. They said the clerk's office should have the order. However, when I called the clerk's office they said the prosecutor's office was in possession of the order. After some back and forth phone calls I came to the conclusion that the order was either lost or misplaced somewhere between the clerk's office and the prosecutor's office, but how does a court order get lost?! I called the clerk's office a third time and asked for a supervisor, explaining the situation and asking if she would personally go through Matt's court file, and try to locate the formal sentencing order.

In the meantime, I gave Matt's attorney's office another call. I didn't think they were being proactive enough. Their office should have made the phone calls I was making on Matt's behalf. I spoke with Mr. Jones, the new young attorney at Mr. Harvey's office who seemed to be handling many of the details of the paperwork involving Matt's case. I asked him what else could be done to get DOC to come for Matt. Mr. Jones' response was that I should probably have Mr. Harvey file a "Writ of Mandamus." He explained to me in very lay terms that a Writ of Mandamus is a petition that would basically compel DOC to come and get Matt. He quoted me the fee that Mr. Harvey's office would charge to prepare and file the Writ. I had no extra money in my budget to pay Mr. Harvey's office to prepare a Writ. I still had my own court fines, and attorney's fees, among other things, to pay.

Mr. Jones told me it was fairly simple to prepare and file a Writ, and in all probability, I could do it myself. He said when completed, I would need to take it to the jail, give it to one of the clerks, explaining that it's legal mail, which required Matt's signature, and ask them to notarize it. Then I would need to bring it to the Circuit Court to be submitted, and it would be faxed immediately to DOC. I thanked him and immediately headed to our public library's law department. I got the correct format for the Writ and read half dozen examples of how to prepare one. Within an hour I typed up a first draft of the Writ of Mandamus, proofread it, and then asked the law librarian to have a look at it. Within a couple hours it was ready for Matt's signature.

In the Writ, I requested DOC to remove Matt from the county jail as soon as possible because of his health, and the amount of weight he had lost. Since the Writ would need Matt's signature, I prayed, and took it to the jail. As I was going into the jail Lauren's attorney, whom I had known for a number of years, was coming out. We stopped and chatted momentarily. I showed him the Writ and asked his opinion. He looked at it for a few minutes, gave me a big hug and said it was just what I needed. I went into the lobby of the jail and spoke to a notary explaining what I needed to have done to the document. She asked me to wait while she took it to Matt, and in less than fifteen minutes it was signed by Matt and I was heading to Circuit Court to file it.

On Monday I called the Clerk's office again and spoke with the supervisor whom I had spoken with the previous week about the missing sentencing order that DOC needed. She informed me that after looking through Matt's file, the sentencing order had been found, still in his file, *unsigned*. She apologized, saying she didn't know how the order had accidentally been placed in the file all those months, unsigned. Hence the reason DOC had not received it and had not come for him. She assured me the person who was probably responsible for misfiling it had already been relieved of her job weeks earlier because her work had been unsatisfactory. Judge Mayfield was no longer at the Circuit Court, but had been reassigned to another court, in another jurisdiction since the judges are periodically rotated. The supervisor said the order would be taken, by courier, to the judge that day, to be signed and then faxed to DOC immediately. I thanked her. Shortly DOC would have both, the Writ of Mandamus, and a signed sentencing order. It was late July, and hopefully now, Matt would soon be moved!! He had been there, in solitary confinement, far too long and had lost far too much weight. I was greatly concerned for his health. David, at least, was not in confinement and was allowed to interact with other inmates and have visitation and letters from us.

I called Matt's attorney's office to give them an update about the sentencing order, and again spoke with Mr. Jones, telling him of the conversation with the clerk, and where the unsigned order had been found. Mr. Jones was furious. He said he would be willing to bet money that the order had not been accidentally left unsigned and placed in the file. He felt it had intentionally been misplaced, by the prosecutors, in order to punish Matt further, and prolong his stay at the jail. I wondered how long the order would have been left unsigned, sitting in Matt's court file, and how long he would have been left in isolation, slowly starving, if I hadn't been persistent.

Although I was angry beyond words at the court and the jail's neglect of Matt's physical condition, I felt such relief in knowing he would be leaving the jail fairly soon. He would be heading to prison, but hopefully the conditions would somehow be better. The Holy Spirit simply said to me, "It's going to be soon now for both your sons." "Thank you, Father God," was my response, "and thank you for teaching me to be persistent when I need to be."

Almost exactly four weeks after the Writ of Mandamus was filed and the formal sentencing order was found, Joanna and Julia were visiting David at the jail one evening and he told them one of the officers informed him that DOC would be coming for him sometime within the next twenty-four hours. I was happy to hear the news but surprised the information had been told to him. For security reasons it is not the policy of the county jail to tell inmates when or where they are being moved, until the morning of the actual move.

The next morning when I went to work I called the jail to ask if David had been moved. The officer informed me that David was still there. I decided to also ask about Matt, expecting her to tell me he was still there, as well. To my incredible surprise, and I think to hers, she told me Matt was gone!! DOC had come for him early on the morning of Friday, August 26, 2005. I was surprised, relieved, teary eyed, happy for him, sad for him, all, at the same time. "Are you certain," I asked her? "Let me double check this for you, Mrs. Smith." She returned to the phone shortly saying, "Yes, Mrs. Smith, Matt is gone, but your other son, David is still here." I thanked her, got off the phone and prayed, "Lord, thank you so much that your hands and your eyes are still on my children, and You, my Lord, will protect them and watch over them wherever they go. Thank you, Father."

That day, I must have called the jail at least four times asking various questions, and each time confirming that Matt was gone. I prayed all day for him, for the favor and mercy of God to go with him, and for divine protection over him. I was physically at work but mentally and spiritually, my thoughts were elsewhere.

Where had they taken him? When could we see him and talk to him? Would he want to see me? Those questions were continuously in my thoughts. I called Mr. Harvey's office to let them know, and asked them to try and find out where he had been taken. They said since it was Friday, they would not know until Monday. I called my pastor and my daughters to tell them it was not David who was moved, but Matt. I did not call James, since he was at work, and I didn't want to distract him. However, by the time we both got home from work, James already knew. A friend of James' who worked at the jail called and told him, and also told him where Matt had been taken, but James couldn't remember the name of the facility. He said he simply focused on the fact that Matt was finally gone from the jail and would no longer be in isolation, unable to have visitors or get mail. We prayed the food would be better, wherever he was being taken, and he would begin to eat again and gain some weight.

That evening as I continued to pray and intercede, Sharon, from the intercessory prayer team at church called me. It was an answer to my prayers. "Diana, you will never guess whom I heard from today. Matt!!" Matt had called her and asked her to please get a message to me since our phone was still not back on. He told her he had been taken to a processing center, about two hours from our home. He asked her to tell me he loved me, and he knew he had messed up his life by making some horrible choices. I felt an immense sense of relief somehow, knowing where he had been taken, and not having to wait an entire weekend for his attorney to find out for me. Matt would be at the processing center a couple of weeks and then moved to the penitentiary. We had no way of knowing which prison he would be housed at, or how far it would be from our home.

Early on Monday, August 29th, I decided to call the jail again, before I left for work, to check on David, because I had a feeling David was going to be right behind Matt in being moved. Indeed that was the case. The officer whom I spoke with confirmed what I knew in my heart, even before I made the call. Yes, David was gone, too. DOC had come for him early that morning. I dropped to my knees and began to pray. I hurt for both of them. I had to pray in the spirit and ask the Holy Spirit to compose me and give me peace. My two oldest sons were heading to the penitentiary! It was beyond anything I could ever have imagined for my children. As I prayed for the Holy Spirit to put His hands on my sons, watch over them, and sustain them for the journey ahead, I knew He was also sustaining me. A peace and calmness began to wash over me and quiet my spirit. I began to feel an assurance in my spirit, knowing that God is still in control, and nothing takes Him by surprise, or catches Him off guard. God isn't scratching His head and wondering what to do next when we make incredibly bad choices that alter the course of our lives. I knew He would be with each of my sons.

Several days after Matt and David were taken by DOC I went to the jail and picked up a small bag of their personal possessions which they were not allowed to take to prison.

Although Matt had not been allowed to send or receive mail while he was at the jail, my pastor had suggested I continue writing to him. We knew his letters were being held by the jail in a storage bin, and would be given to him when he was taken to prison. Usually every time I wrote David, I also wrote Matt. Sometimes I wrote to them several times in a week. In every letter I would encourage them to continue to pray and trust God. I would let them know that we continued each day to pray and intercede for them, and they are loved, missed and thought of every single day.

After I found out which prison processing centers Matt and David were sent to, I wrote them telling them we wanted to come see them as soon as they would be allowed to have visitors. On the same day I mailed their letters, I received a letter from David. I was delighted to hear from him.

From David's letter I realized he didn't know Matt had been taken from the jail three days before him. However, my eyes immediately zoomed in on the sentence in his letter saying he was in "the hole" (isolation) because he had gotten a charge for refusing to get his hair cut. I had warned him several times when he was still at the jail that it would be mandatory to have his hair cut. It was not an option. He understood that. However, he still refused to get his hair cut, had been given a charge for "refusing to cooperate," put in isolation, and his hair had been cut anyway! Worst, his visitation privilege, while at the processing center, was terminated! How foolish we can sometimes be! In his letter he said, "Mom, don't worry about me. Even though I am in the hole, I am fine. I have my Bible, a pencil and paper. I have Jesus, and I am at peace with Him. We will get to see each other when I leave the processing center in a couple of weeks. They haven't told me yet which prison they will be sending me to but I will let you know as soon as I know." Immediately I wrote him back.

15

THE LONG ROAD AHEAD

Two weeks after I had written to Matt at the processing center, I still had not heard back from him. A friend said I should not write him but give him time to adjust to the new environment. I felt he needed to know we still loved him, and he greatly needed encouragement. I wanted him to remember that God forgives every sin and transgression. There was a chance he would still be angry with me, and still of great concern to me was the fact that he might not want to see me, and might not put me on his visitation list. My friend said, "What if he's just tearing up your letters, Diana? He might not even be reading all those letters you are sending him." I rebuked those words and every negative thought that came to my mind. I continued to write Matt and encourage him to seek the Lord. I knew I would always pray for him and David, and tell them they are loved and greatly missed.

I called the processing center and spoke to a counselor assigned to Matt. She said Matt relayed to her that he was not yet ready to have visitors, but would make up his visitation list when he felt ready. I tried to accept that and not be anxious.

Sometime later Matt made up his visitation list and my name was on the list. I was excited and happy that we would be able to visit him. At the same time I was nervous about what his reaction would be to me when we were able to sit face to face and talk. The fact that he had included me on his visitation list was a good indicator that he was at least willing to see me and talk.

I prayed much during the week for the upcoming visit to go well. I prayed we would be candid with each other, and he would say what he felt he needed to say to me. I wanted to allow him to vent those feelings and ask the questions he must have wanted to ask me since I revealed the money which had been buried on our property. I asked friends and family to pray before we went for the visit.

On Saturday, September 24th, 2005, four days after Matt made up his visitation list, Joanna, Julia, James and I piled into the car and made a two and a half hour trip to see him at the processing center. The last time Joanna and Julia had seen Matt in person had been over two years. The last time James and I saw Matt had been eleven months earlier, in October, 2004 in court, when he was formally sentenced.

When we arrived at the facility we were only permitted to bring in our driver's license and a ten dollar roll of quarters to purchase snacks out of the vending machines. Each visitor went into a room with an officer of their sex to be searched.

After being processed in the four of us stood talking quietly waiting to be taken into the actual visitation room. We faced a large window with iron bars overlooking a huge fenced yard. As we stood there I noticed a bald, clean shaven young man standing alone in the yard, facing us, and apparently waiting to be allowed to come into the building we were in. My eyes fixed on him for some curious reason. There was something about his mannerisms that was familiar. I stared hard for another moment, and though we were all looking out of that window, I was the first to realize we were looking at Matt! Excitedly I said, "That's Matt! He has shaved his head." "Are you sure, Mom?" Joanna asked. "Yes, yes, I'm sure, Joanna. Watch him closely for a moment. Notice his mannerisms." A moment later Joanna laughed and said, "Yes, it is, and he looks so much like Dad standing there." We had never seen Matt with all of his hair shaven off. I turned to look at James who was standing behind Julia, with both hands shoved deeply into his pockets. For a brief moment I saw such pain and sadness in James' eyes that I had to look away, or I would have begun to cry. I knew what he was thinking and feeling, because I felt and thought the same thing. "God, why did this have to happen? What a senseless, tremendous waste of a young, talented life. God, can you ever, somehow, use this incredible mess that has disrupted and forever changed far too many lives? Can You somehow use all of this pain, hurt, humiliation and brokenness to Your honor and glory, to make us stronger, wiser, more compassionate and caring human beings? Can you, Lord?" Those were rhetorical questions in my mind, and yet I knew the answer was absolutely, yes. God can, and God would use all of it. Not one tear would be wasted. Silently, I reminded myself again, I was not going to cry today in front of Matt.

Suddenly the door was buzzed and Matt came from the yard into the building. He almost directly faced us as he entered, though a glass window and bars separated us. He did not see us initially. He was quickly shown into another room which had another large glass window to our left. That room appeared to be the holding room for inmates. As he went into that room he walked right up to the window between him and us. He looked directly at us, and seemed somewhat surprised to see us. I placed my hand on the glass, as if to touch his face, and smiled at him. He smiled a slight smile and nodded his head to us. Momentarily he moved away from the window, and then in another minute he came back and looked again, as if to be sure we were really there. I saw the same sadness in his eyes that I saw in James' but to an even greater depth. He darted away from the window again and sat down with the other men in the room. Now it was our turn to be moved into the visitor's room. We presented our passes to the guard at the desk and were shown to a small plastic table with five chairs around it.

The room was full of visitors, in small groups, talking, laughing and embracing. After we were seated we all seemed to focus on the door, in the corner, that we knew Matt would walk through. Quickly the door opened and the first inmate came out. There seemed to be a long pause, as we waited anxiously, and then Matt emerged. We all stood simultaneously, unrehearsed, as he came toward us. I was the first to step toward him and wrap my arms around him. I don't recall saying anything to him at first. I just remember reaching up and hugging him. Joanna and Julia quickly joined in. Matt wrapped his arms around all three of us, as we embraced him for a long moment. There were no tears, no words at first, just hugs. We told him that he looked wonderful. James waited for us to step back, and then he and Matt clasped hands and hugged. Matt looked older with his clean shaven head and thin, neat mustache. He was still extremely thin for someone almost six feet tall, but to my delight he looked healthy, not emaciated or sickly. He said he was slowly beginning to regain his physical strength and that he had gained a couple of pounds in the few weeks he had been there. He asked about David, and many others. We talked for almost two hours. More accurately, we let him talk and we responded.

I noticed even with as much as he had been through, some things thankfully remained the same in his personality, in particular his sense of humor and his ability to make other people laugh. That was a positive thing in this negative environment. As we sat with him, there were moments that we laughed so much I almost forgot where we were. We laughed about some of the silly and immature things he had seen some of the inmates do, including himself. We laughed as he described himself with boiled eggs hidden in his socks, taken from the cafeteria, so he'd have something to eat later. He had gotten caught just outside the cafeteria when he was being checked. Thankfully there was no punishment for being caught with the boiled eggs. The eggs were simply taken and thrown in the trash can.

There were also moments, as he spoke, that I could not forget where we were, and I had to hold back the tears, remembering I had promised myself I would not cry that day, in front of Matt. One such moment was when he described seeing two men fighting on the recreation yard, while the guards watched instead of breaking it up, until the loser was pretty bloodied up. He said the men told him it's the unwritten code to stay out of other people's fights.

We were reminded that this was a prison processing center or a stopping off point for Matt, where DOC classifies prisoners at various "levels" ranging from level-one minimum security, to level-five maximum security. We did not know it then, but Matt had already been classified as a level-five inmate.

During our visit Matt asked questions I knew he was going to ask. "Mom, why did you tell the police there was money on our property? What purpose did you think it would serve?" James gave me a look that said, "I told you Mom. You did a stupid thing to reveal that money!" I took a deep breath before answering and prayed silently, "Lord, help me to say what you've told me to say." Then I responded, "Matt, I did it because I knew it was the right thing to do. The money did not belong to any of us. I knew the Lord wanted me to be honest, and I knew I needed to be obedient to what the Spirit of God was encouraging me to do. If I had not been obedient to God's leading I would not have peace. I also knew if I didn't we would continue to be watched, since the detectives had already suspected money was still on our property. They would have come when they felt like it, disrupting our lives, just as Ms. O'Hara said, and I did not wish to live like that. Also, none of us would have been safe, had word of the money leaked out to the wrong person. Matt, I ask you to please forgive me that I hurt you by betraying your confidence. For that I am sorry; but I have no regrets about revealing the money and getting it off our property. I believe each one of us, throughout this entire situation, did what we felt in our hearts we needed to do." Matt didn't comment. Instead, he changed the conversation.

Too soon our visitation time was over and visitors were asked to move to one side of the room and inmates to the other side. I noticed many of the visitors left the place they were standing and went to the inmate for one last hug. We were no exception. The guards didn't seem to mind. We all hugged Matt and told him again how much we love and pray for him and David each day. We embraced him until we had to start walking through the door to leave the visitation area. It would be almost a year before we would see him again.

On the trip returning home we were all quiet. Each of us seemed preoccupied with our own thoughts. As I reflected on the visit, I felt it was a bitter-sweet time. It was wonderful to be with him, encourage him, talk, hug him, and remind him that he and David are never, ever forgotten. More importantly, it was a time to remind him that God forgives all of our sins and transgressions if we will confess to Him. There was definitely the inevitable sadness of having to leave him. He and David's absences in our lives were the constant daily reality of this entire situation. I was ever reminded of the incalculable loss to all who had been involved, not just my family.

We were now anxious for David to be moved from the processing center, since he was unable to have visitors while there. When David was finally moved from the processing center he was moved to a level-two minimum security facility about two hours from our home. We were equally excited to be able to go see him. David's oldest son, Daniel was then six years old and we took him with us on the first visit to see David. Daniel was not the child David had with Beatrice, but with another young woman, before his marriage to Beatrice. It had been over a year and a half since Daniel had seen David. Daniel, who is normally a reserved and quiet child, was almost unable to contain himself with joy at the idea of going to see his Dad. "Grandma, I'm going to hug Daddy so tightly and I'm going to sit on his lap for a long time and tell him how much I love and miss him."

When we arrived at the prison I was pleasantly surprised to see inmates dressed in jeans and light blue shirts. It was certainly less shocking for the children to see someone dressed that way, rather than the brightly colored orange jump suits. There were many women sitting quietly in the visitation area with small children on their laps waiting for husbands, boyfriends, brothers and dads. As I looked around the room my heart went out to all the families impacted by the incarceration process and the toll it unarguably takes on each family member economically, socially, spiritually, emotionally; and who can even begin to calculate the profound impact it has on the lives of our children?!

Daniel and I could not sit still. We both stood watching the door David would walk through momentarily to come into the visitation area. As soon as David emerged through the door I said to Daniel, "There is your Dad." Daniel ran toward David as fast as his six year old legs could carry him. David bent down and scooped him up in his arms. Both of them grinned from ear to ear, hugging and kissing each other. We all wrapped our arms around David. He looked well. His long, thick black hair was gone, and instead he wore a low cut style. He looked older, wiser, and still so handsome. He looked peaceful, and not in the least bit stressed. That kind of peace only comes from the Lord.

Daniel positioned himself comfortably on David's lap, grinning from ear to ear, with arms wrapped around David's neck as if he would never let go. We asked David lots of questions about the facility and what his daily routine consisted of. He talked about the food, the guards, other inmates, and of course he inquired about our visit to see Matt. He asked James and me how we were adjusting and managing at home. He asked about Beatrice and his youngest son, Joshua. He had not heard from her and she was not responding to any of his letters.

David told us he had applied for and received a job in the prison library, which he was enjoying. In addition, he had taken it upon himself to help some of the men who wanted to obtain their GED, by tutoring them. We talked about the educational opportunities that facility offered, in order for him to take some college level classes. He said he already knew he wanted to take some college courses and that a local community college worked in conjunction with the prison facility, offering college credit classes toward earning an Associate's Degree. I was delighted to hear that, and encouraged him wholeheartedly. He went on to say that he did not think he would qualify for any financial aid through the prison. If he took college credit classes, he would have to have private, outside funding to pay for the classes. We prayed with him and told him we believed God would provide for him to be able to take the college credit classes. We encouraged him to get all the information and keep us posted about what he would need.

After we talked for a while, I once again apologized to David profusely, with all of my heart, because I felt if it had it not been for me and Matt, and the decisions we each made, David would not have been in this place. I felt David had been dealt an extremely unfair hand by the court. What truly amazed me was that David, contrary to Matt, was not bitter, or angry with anyone; not with me, or the prosecutors, not with anyone. In the midst of me apologizing to him, he stopped me and said, "Mom, please stop apologizing. I am not angry with you or anyone else. God has seen fit to allow this to happen, for whatever reason, and in all of this, He has been merciful to me. If I had still been out there, I'd probably be dead by now. You see, I was using some pretty serious drugs." I listened to his honest confession. I did not judge him or condemn him. I listened and then put my arms around him and told him God can and will restore what Satan had tried to steal away from him and each one of us. I was so thankful that he had the courage to be honest with me.

In retrospect, as David was speaking, I had to be honest with myself and admit I had certainly seen signs of him using drugs long before he had been arrested. However, when I had questioned him several times, years earlier, and others about that possibility, it was always denied, so I had dismissed my suspicions. As I listened to David speaking, I, too, saw the mercy of God in his life, as well as in Matt's. I wondered if Matt now saw the mercy of God in his life, as David saw it in his, and as I saw more clearly each day, in all of our lives! I was happy that in the last couple of weeks we had been able to sit down, face to face, with both Matt and David. I felt those visits, and the conversations, would somehow help with the healing and forgiveness process in each one of us.

Several weeks after we had visited Matt at the processing center he was moved to the prison where he would be housed for the next five years. I was not prepared for how far they would send him. He was sent to a level-five, maximum security facility, far into the mountains, nine hours from our home. At level-five the men are confined, or "warehoused" twenty three hours of the day to a small cell which they share with another man. It truly seems inhumane! On my budget there would be no way we would be able to visit him monthly or even regularly. It would mean an overnight, weekend trip, with eighteen hours of total driving time.

Months passed again before we heard from Matt after he was taken to the level-five facility. When I called, his new counselor said Matt did not want us to travel there until spring-time because they were already having a significant amount of snow. The counselor said Matt still needed to make up his visitation list for that facility and he said he would not be making it up until spring of the following year.

Spring, 2006 came and Matt made up his visitation list. However, it would be the fall of that year before we would be financially able to go see him. The most reliable vehicle we had was my little Ford Escort. In addition to me, Julia, Joanna, and James there would now be Joanna's husband who would make the trip to see Matt. Joanna had gotten married a year earlier.

We were determined to go see Matt, so on Labor Day weekend the five of us crammed into the little Ford Escort to make the trip. The ride was long and uncomfortable, but no one complained.

I cried when we arrived at the facility. It looked as if someone had sliced off the top of a mountain and put a maximum security prison in the middle of nowhere. I cried when I hugged him, and for the first twenty minutes of our visit, as guards closely watched us. Visitation at this facility was totally different from our visit with him a year ago at the processing center. Here he sat on one side of a long table with other inmates, and we sat on the opposite side of the table with other visitors. We were not permitted to reach across the table to touch him until our visit was complete. I cried again when visitation was over, and for an hour after we left him.

There was such a stark contrast between the level-five facility and the level-two facility where David was housed. At level-two the men are not housed in cells, but rather in large, open rooms with numerous bunk beds. They are allowed freedom of movement within that room throughout the day. At level-two there is a tremendous amount of emphasis on inmates bettering themselves through education. There is light at the end of their tunnels because most of the men in level-two facilities are going to get out. At the level-five facilities, where men have been given life and multiple life sentences, there is little emphasis on education or trade/skill classes because the states don't see the need to spend the money to teach them a skill, since most of them will not return to society.

For the next five years our visits to see Matt were, at most, twice a year. After our first visit we decided that for future trips to see Matt we would rent a larger, more comfortable vehicle. Although our visits to see Matt were not as often as those to see David, we wrote to both of them weekly. We did not hear from Matt as often as David. Matt, thankfully, understood why we were not able to come see him as often. Still it pained me greatly to not be able to visit him as often as I wished we could.

About a year after Matt had been moved so far away, I began writing, praying, and making phone calls to DOC and any elected officials who might be able to convince DOC to move Matt closer to home. It presented such a hardship for the family to visit him. In the meantime, we found a church an hour away from our home that allowed us to have DOC approved video visits with Matt. That helped, because we could see him, but nothing took the place of an in-person visit.

I would be lying if I said I didn't worry about my sons, although I tried hard not to. I reminded myself constantly to put my hope and trust continuously in the Lord. Every time a worried thought came to mind, I would say, "Lord, I give this thought to You. Thank You for protecting both of them each day. Oh, God!" God's Word says in First Peter 5:7 we are to cast all our cares upon Him because He care for us. I was determined to do that, and some days it took focused effort to cast those worried thoughts over on the Lord.

One day when I was praying for Matt and David the Holy Spirit began instructing me to pray for "a heart transplant for Matt." A heart transplant, I thought?! Almost immediately I knew what the Holy Spirit meant. I needed to begin praying for the Lord to change Matt's heart from a heart that was bitter, angry, hurt, and resentful, to a heart that was forgiving and filled with the peace of God. Ezekiel 36:26 says, "I will give you a new heart and put a new spirit in you. I will remove from you the heart of stone and give you a heart of flesh." I knew God was going to do that for Matt.

In the meantime, David was able to sign up for college classes and he began working toward an Associate's Degree. By faith we believed we would be able to pay for the costs of his classes between me, Joanna, and James contributing, and truly God provided. Sometimes our church family would even pay a semester's tuition for David.

Several months after Matt was taken to the level five-facility there was a front page story in our newspaper about Matt's former girlfriend, Lauren. She was being sought, nationwide, by the police, and had been indicted by a special Grand Jury in our area. The article said she was suspected of running a "large scale cocaine operation."

Like Matt, Lauren had been given numerous opportunities to turn her life in a positive direction, but each time she had chosen to get more deeply involved in the drug business. Now she was back in the system.

In mid-January, 2006, Lauren's picture was on the front page of our local newspaper. She and several others had been found and arrested in another state, hundreds of miles from our area, in possession of a large quantity of drugs. Lauren really did have her hands just as deeply in the dirt as Debbie and Sarah had all along suspected.

Lauren and several other young people were extradited back to our state to stand trial. I felt so sad for her because I was fairly certain Lauren was going to prison this time, and I suspected her sentence was not going to be an easy one.

Six months later Lauren, who was then twenty years old, received a forty year sentence for drug trafficking. The court mercifully suspended twenty five years of her time, leaving her fifteen to serve. Under current law in this state she will serve eighty percent of her time. I have asked myself, "When young people get involved in the lifestyle of selling and using drugs, do they really count the cost? Is the price that each person ultimately pays worth the risk they take?" I think not! Words could not express how badly I felt for Lauren and the other young people.

David, in addition to taking college credit classes, working in the prison library, and tutoring men in his dorm, was also involved in a Bible study with some of the men. I was so proud of the effort he was making to better himself. During the next five years that David was in prison neither Beatrice, nor her family ever visited him. I continued to pray for Beatrice.

David continued to grow in his relationship with Jesus Christ. It was obvious in his letters and in the conversations we had with him that he was growing in leaps and bounds spiritually. I was delighted to see what God was doing in him.

When David completed his Associates Degree, he took numerous other classes, many of which were offered free to the men, such as HVAC, (heating, ventilation and air conditioning), Building Maintenance, and Plumbing. He received many certifications and achievement awards while in prison. He stayed focused and busy until the day he walked out, as a free man again, and thankfully that focus and determination has continued in him.

One day, a couple of years before David came home, and much to my surprise and delight, Beatrice got in touch with me, and we talked. We really talked, and both of us forgave the other, and decided to let the past be the past. None of us have the power to change the past, but we can affect the future by the decisions that we make today. Beatrice began to bring my grandson, Joshua, to the house again and our family began to build a relationship with that precious child, once more. I had been praying for several years by then for that situation. God indeed is a hearer and an answerer of prayers.

In 2010, five months before David's scheduled release from prison, he and Beatrice corresponded, and she told him she wanted a divorce. It was not a surprise to any of us. David had continued wearing his wedding band all those years, and did so until after his divorce was final. Still, I am thankful to God that Beatrice and I made peace and forgave each other.

Beatrice's loss, when David went to jail and to prison, can never be minimized. Her losses were monumental. I have always understood that and hurt deeply for her.

16

WITH CHRIST WE CONTINUE THE JOURNEY

More than a decade has passed since we went to jail and David and Matt went to prison. David was released from prison in September, 2010. He served a little more than six years. Matt is still incarcerated. However, he has been moved to a lower level facility, closer to home, and we are able to visit him much more often. It is my firm belief that he will one day be allowed to come home, a free man. I know he will be changed and a far better person, totally sold out for Christ.

Although I would never, ever want to go through what we went through, the deeper relationship that each of us has forged with Christ and the lessons learned from our experiences are priceless. In the years that have followed each of us has grown, become stronger, and continued to heal.

Six months after I came home from jail and after briefly having two minimum paying jobs I started a residential cleaning business. Ten years later, as I reflect back on the decision to start a business, I will say it has been one of the best decisions I've ever made. It has allowed me to have an incredible amount of flexibility in my day to day schedule.

When David got out of prison he came back to live at home for a short time. He enrolled in college to continue his education and was blessed to be re-hired at his old job. Within one week of being home he was able to get his driver's license back. We serve an awesome God!! Less than a year later he was accepted at an excellent university in a nearby city to pursue a degree in Engineering.

Almost three years later, in 2013, David was invited back to the prison to deliver the Commencement Address for a class of several hundred men who were graduating. Many of the men received their GEDs, some received their Associate's Degree, and others received various types of certifications. I had the privilege of going with David that day and hearing him deliver the Commencement Address. What an honor to see my son, who was once an inmate at the facility, delivering the Commencement Address!! I cried happy tears that day. We knew it was truly the favor of God which made such an opportunity possible.

David was truly blessed to be have been housed at a state prison that allowed its inmates to select from a wide variety of vocational programs and apprenticeship training, in addition to the post-secondary educational programs offered by one of the local community colleges. Not all state prisons or prisoners are as fortunate.

In spite of the fact that David, James and I have a felony, God continues to open many doors of opportunity for each of us. We are blessed to serve a God who is full of mercy and compassion for His children, no matter what we have done.

James, too, has truly been blessed since that time. He initially started a commercial cleaning business then eventually returned to college, with encouragement from family and friends. He first obtained an Associate's Degree, then a Bachelor's Degree from an excellent university, and is currently completing work on his Master's Degree. God continues to open many excellent doors of opportunity for James beyond anything we could have asked, or imagined, or hoped for.

Both James and David have become strong Christian men, and it has given me the greatest joy to see them continuously growing in faith and in relationship with Jesus Christ each day.

Joanna obtained her Bachelor's and Master's Degrees and began a career in teaching. She has continued to travel extensively, internationally. Joanna is also a committed Christian.

Julia became the mother of a precious little boy, whom we adore. She is a hardworking, single, Christian mother and such a blessing to our family.

Since Matt has been moved closer to where we live, we are now able to visit him much more often. This came about because of praying, writing letters to DOC, and more praying. Finally, his name was placed on DOC's "waiting to be moved" list. We found out that names sometimes stay on the list for years before an inmate is moved, and sometimes they are never moved. It's critical that the family of the inmate is persistent and prayerful. However, God has a right timing in all things and one morning as I was praying and having quiet time with the Lord, I felt the Lord speak to my heart to once again write a letter to DOC about Matt being moved. That very day I wrote and mailed yet another letter requesting that Matt be moved closer to home. Within six days of writing and mailing that letter, one of numerous that I had written, Matt was moved to a facility less than two hours from home. I was delighted!! It is my prayer that I will always be obedient to the Lord, in the big things and in the small things, and make the time each day to listen and hear His voice when He speaks in that "still small voice." Time spent in the presence of God is time wisely and well spent. We serve an awesome God, who never changes and still specializes in things thought impossible. He continues to speak to hearts, lives, and impossible situations as we continue to seek Him and listen.

I have seen a gradual, but continuous, growth in Matt in the past few years. It is only with God's help that Matt is changing into the man God has always desired him to be. I believe Matt is still accepting the fact that Christ has forgiven him, and he must learn to forgive himself. Just because a person commits a terrible crime does not mean that person is hopeless or beyond God's reach and forgiveness. The late Chuck Colson of Prison Fellowship once said, "We believe that no life is beyond the reach of God's redemptive power." How true!

As I have said many times, the sentence Matt was given was an "over the top" amount of time for the crime. However, we cannot change yesterday or dwell in the past. Isaiah 43:18 tells us not to dwell there. It is my hope and prayer that Matt will develop a profound relationship with the Living God and have an awesome testimony of God's grace, mercy, love, healing and forgiveness in his life.

In the midst of the greatest pain and turmoil of our lives so much changed for our family, but God was always there, constantly constant! Never did He leave nor forsake us (Hebrews 13:5), even when I didn't feel like He was there; He was there! His love for us continues to be unchanging, unwavering, and unconditional. He has truly been the anchor for my soul (Hebrews 6:19).

If we allow the Spirit of God to work in us, in spite of our pain and brokenness, if we yield to His Holy Spirit, then we will come through the ordeal a more caring and compassionate human being. Changed? Yes! Absolutely! But, if we don't allow the Spirit of God to work in us, to heal us, to teach us how to forgive those who have hurt us, then we become the walking wounded, bitter, spiritually crippled, and unable to move forward in our lives. For a while I am certain that I was "the walking wounded" because I allowed Satan to hold me captive behind the prison doors of guilt and shame. However, I can't say it enough, that it doesn't matter what you've done, whether you've been a drug dealer, murderer, thief, liar, prostitute, adulterer, or whatever; Jesus came to set the captive free, and whom the Son sets free is free indeed!

Martin Luther, the great theologian, born in Germany in 1483, once said, "I have held many things in my hands and I have lost them all, but the things I have given to God, those are the things I still possess." I purpose each day to give everything and everyone in my life to God.

People have said that "time is the healer" but "time" was never the healer for me, since the hardest thing for me was to forgive myself and let go of the past, the pain, the hurt, bitterness, humiliation and disappointment; all the things I could not change. I was able to forgive everyone else, but I struggled with forgiving myself. Whatever I did, wrong or right, I had to take full responsibility for. The Healer for me (and for you) was God and His Word; going to Him daily, and sometimes many times daily, giving all of my pain and woundedness to Him.

Eventually, and lastly, I also had to admit that I was angry with Matt, and I had to forgive him, as well. "Lord, I forgive Matt for the horrible choices he made which will profoundly impact the remainder of his life and the lives of numerous others. I forgive him for the enormous pain, hurt and humiliation he has caused not only our family, but so many others whose lives are forever changed."

It has become clearer to me with each passing day that the choices which we make, or the "watershed turns," have so much to do with the shaping of our character and who we allow ourselves to become. Never allow Satan's or anyone else's accusations against you to define who you are, no matter what your past experience has been. Always remember who God says you are. What I did and where I was for four months does not define who I am in Christ.

Satan's intent is always to stop us, to paralyze us with shame and destroy us because of the unwise and foolish decisions we make. However, the Word of God says, what Satan meant for bad in your life, what Satan meant to destroy you, God will use for His honor and glory and for our growth, maturity and development (paraphrase from Genesis 50:20). As Christians, we know God forgives all of our sins and transgressions, even though we reap the consequences of our sins and choices by having to live with those choices every day.

We need to repent of sin quickly. A pastor once said, "Sin will either cause God to move away from us, or us to move away from God."

Sometimes when I start trying to dwell in the past again and I think of all that happened and feel like having a "pity-party" I remind myself to focus on God's Word and His truth and not dwell on the past. We have been forgiven and washed clean by the awesome and precious blood of Jesus. I am determined to give all honor and glory to God, and to be the salt and light in the world that He calls each of His children to be.

Lastly, please remember that our words have power not only to convey information, but Proverbs 18:21 says, "The power of life and death are in the tongue." Therefore, as born again children of the Most High God we can speak faith or doubt, life or death, blessings or cursing over our situations, our lives, our health, our children, etcetera. Scripture also says (Proverbs 23:7, Amplified Bible), "For as he thinks in his heart, so he is." If you think you are defeated you will begin to talk and act like you are defeated, and you will be; but if you remember that no matter what, you are a victorious overcomer by the blood of the Lamb and the word of your testimony (Revelation 12:11, paraphrased), you will NOT be defeated.

May the peace, blessings and wisdom of the Lord Jesus Christ fill your heart and life, in spite of life's challenges and changes, as you embrace God's unconditional love. Everything in the natural realm is subject to change, even the facts, but God's Word never changes because Hebrews 13:8 says, "Jesus is the same yesterday, today and forever."

A FEW INCARCERATION FACTS

The NAACP Criminal Justice Fact Sheet, 2014 (www.naacp.
org):

- The United States makes up five percent of the world's
  population but has twenty –five percent of the world's
  prisoners.
- African Americans now constitute nearly one million of
  the 2.3 million incarcerated.
- African Americans are incarcerated at nearly six times the
  rate of Whites.
- In 2008, African Americans and Hispanics comprised
  58% of all prisoners in the United States.

The International Center for Prison Studies (2013) says, "U.S.
has more people incarcerated than any other country in the world."

**The National Association of State Budget Officers (2011-2013
Report)** says, "U.S. taxpayers spend over $50 billion annually for
state prisons."

**Washington Post, April 30, 2014, article by Emily Badger
entitled "The Meteoric, Costly and Unprecedented Rise of
Incarceration in America" says:**
"Since the 1970s Congress and state legislatures have enacted
a number of changes to prison and sentencing laws that mandate
prison time for lesser offenses. During the 1980s Congress began to enact "mandatory minimum" laws. The 1990s brought the

"three strikes laws." More people were going to jail, carrying longer sentences. As a result, between 1980 and 2010 the incarceration rate for drug crimes increased ten-fold."

The Sentencing Project Research and Advocacy for Reform (2014):

- The United States is the world's leader in incarceration
  with 2.2 million people currently in the nation's prisons or
  jails, which is a 500% increase over the past 30 years.
- Nationally, an estimated 5.85 million Americans are denied the right to vote because of laws that prohibit voting
  by people with felony convictions.
- With regard to juveniles in the justice system, "While re-
  forms are underway in many places, there remains an urgent
  need to reframe our responses to juvenile delinquency."
- The number of woman in prisons, a third of whom are
  incarcerated for drug offenses, is increasing at nearly double the rate for men. These women often have significant
  histories of physical and sexual abuse, high rates of HIV
  infection, and substance abuse. Large-scale women's im-
  prisonment has resulted in an increasing number of children who suffer from their mother's incarceration and the
  loss of family ties.

EPILOGUE

It is my hope that as you have read, *When the Bottom Drops Out of Your Life*, you have been encouraged, informed and motivated. I pray that you have been encouraged to know that no matter what you're going through, God is faithful and always there.

It is my hope that you have been informed about the high incarceration rate of minorities in U.S. prisons; and the fact that we have the highest incarceration rate in the WORLD!! Be informed about the people you elect and put in positions to make laws and decisions which affect every one of us, in particular the current sentencing laws and guidelines that send people to prison for longer periods of time than necessary. We don't necessarily pay attention to the laws until someone we love is in the legal system. Be informed about what you can do to bring about change and make a difference, because there is an urgent need for change in our laws and in our prisons.

Finally, I pray that you will be motivated to be involved, proactive and prayerful for those in prisons who have no voice to speak for themselves. Make phone calls to elected officials, write letters, and send email(s) to assure that the incarcerated are being treated humanely, and are being rehabilitated educationally; and that parole, which has been abolished in some states, is reinstated so some will have the opportunity to return to society again.

In my opinion it would be more reasonable to have laws in the U.S. that are consistent in every state, in particular when it comes to Restoration of Rights and voting privileges for the formerly incarcerated. Currently Maine and Vermont are the only two states that allow people with a felony conviction to vote from prison. If all prisoners could vote I can only imagine how the pendulum would quickly swing in this country to bring about prison reform.

NOTES

Chapter 1
Taken from, *DEAR GOD, IT'S ME AND IT'S URGENT,*
Copyright 2008 by Marion Stroud. Used by permission of
Discovery House Publishers
Grand Rapids, Michigan 49501. All rights reserved

Chapter 6
Taken from, *IN THE GRIP OF GRACE,*
Copyright 1996 by Max Lucado. Used by permission of Thomas
Nelson Publishing
Nashville, Tennessee

Chapter 7
Taken from, *LORD, I NEED ANSWERS*
Rerelease of *Lord, Help Me Grow Spiritually Strong in 28 days*
Copyright 2009 by Kay Arthur and David Arthur
Published by Harvest House Publishers
Eugene, Oregon 97402
www.harvesthousepublishers.com
Used by Permission

Chapter 7
Taken from, *BELIEVER'S VOICE OF VICTORY,* Kenneth
Copeland
Article entitled, "Revival is Rattling the Prison Walls," by Kenneth
Copeland at the
Washington, D.C. Victory Campaign on February 3, 1994,

Believer's Voice of Victory Magazine
Harrison House Publishers
Tulsa, Oklahoma

Chapter 16
Prison Fellowship, Mission Statement…"We believe that no life is beyond the reach of God's power…"

Chapter 16
Historically attributed to: Martin Luther, the German Theologian, born 1483
"I have held many things in my hands and I have lost them all, but the things I have given to God, those are the things that I still possess."